all my
Fault

all my Fault

*The true story of a sadistic father
and a little girl left destroyed*

AUDREY DELANEY

EBURY
PRESS

5 7 9 10 8 6 4

Published in 2011 by Ebury Press, an imprint of Ebury Publishing
A Random House Group company
First published in Ireland by Maverick House Publishers in 2008

The Random House Group Limited Reg. No. 954009

Addresses for companies within the Random House Group can be found
at www.randomhouse.co.uk

A CIP catalogue record for this book is available from the British Library

The Random House Group Limited supports The Forest Stewardship
Council (FSC), the leading international forest certification organisation.
All our titles that are printed on Greenpeace approved FSC certified
paper carry the FSC logo. Our paper procurement policy can be found at
www.rbooks.co.uk/environment

Mixed Sources

Product group from well-managed
forests and other controlled sources
www.fsc.org   Cert no. TT-COC-2139
© 1996 Forest Stewardship Council

FSC

Printed in the UK by CPI Cox & Wyman, Reading, RG1 8EX

ISBN 9780091938499

To buy books by your favourite authors and register for offers visit
www.rbooks.co.uk

With my warmest inner heart and spirit, and with the greatest love, I dedicate this book to my son Tyrone (my chipmunk) and to my daughter Robin (my angel). They are the reason I went as far as I could, to do the best for them. I get my strength from the love I feel for them and from them.

This book is also dedicated to my stepdaughter Dee, who is my friend and family; for her encouragement and ability to be my rock many, many times. She shows and tells me how much she loves me every time we are together. She is a credit to herself and her own mother.

Author's Note

This book is a true story, and everything that is recounted in it happened. Some of the information contained in this book is taken from evidence given in the Dublin Circuit Criminal Court. For the sake of privacy, some names have been changed. These appear in italics.

On a personal note, I would like to say that I was compelled to write this story; it was a driven force in me that would not rest until I did it.

This book was written over hundreds of hours and several months, so it was not done lightly, but with passion and motivation to help accomplish the following:

- To help people open their eyes and see how this crime affects children through to adulthood, if they make it that far.
- To show it can be dealt with; without shame.
- To urge families involved in this type of situation to get support to help them deal with it.

- To help teach people to educate their children about what's appropriate and what's not amongst the ones they love and trust.

- To help educate people to recognise someone who is being abused, so they might ask the right questions.

- To make child abuse an issue of public debate.

- To give information to those working with abused children/adults on how it can disturb one's mental health, so that healing can begin.

- To give comfort to all those who have ever been wronged. It was not you; it was the person who did it to you. It is their shame . . . and those who protect them.

Prologue

I was sitting in my little pink car one day with the radio blaring, allowing the music to drown out my thoughts, and pull me into a sweet state of nothingness. I didn't want to think about anything, or feel anything. The music gradually faded and the news came on, slowly reaching into my consciousness.

I only half listened as the newsreader went through the top stories of the day. It was only when I heard the words 'child abuse' that I jolted upwards and froze. Every bone in my body tensed up and I felt my fists clenching involuntarily. The words had struck a chord with me. I tried to push them out of my mind and pretend I hadn't heard them. But it was too late. A door had been opened somewhere in my mind—one that I had sealed shut a very long time ago.

I found myself short of breath, and I had a sense of falling into a black void. I sat in the car for what seemed like an eternity, waiting for the music to wash over me again, to wash away the bad memories. This time, though, it wasn't working; the memories pushed against me, uninvited and unwanted.

I gradually allowed myself to absorb what these words meant. Child sex abuse. When I heard those words I felt like a thousand wasps were crawling all over me body and stinging me all at the one time. The words drilled a hole in my subconscious that caused toxic thoughts to leak out into the rest of my mind. I wanted to put my head under one of the tyres of my car and get someone to drive over it. I just wanted to be put out of my misery. I felt lower than I'd ever felt before.

At first, I denied any connection between me and those hateful words. This was not what happened to me.

My da didn't do that. My da wouldn't do that.

No, it was different. What my da did was completely different.

Sure, it wasn't me da anyway. It was me. It was my fault. There was something dirty about me.

Chapter One

Da was, in many ways, a success story. He came from abject poverty, growing up in a tenement building in Gardiner Street, which runs through the heartland of Dublin's north inner city.

He shared a two-bedroom house with his four siblings and his parents. The place was cold and damp and they often found themselves with barely enough food to feed the family. They shared the one loo with three other floors of tenement residents and had little or nothing to their name, or so I was told.

Gardiner Street had a bad reputation at the time. It was considered a rough street and Da was always very conscious of this growing up. He became so ashamed of having been reared there that he hardly ever admitted it to anyone. In fact, when I was growing up I was never allowed to tell anyone where he was from, even though Nanny and Granddad Delaney were still living there.

Da left school when he was 12 years old, but after he got married he went back to college and studied to become an accountant. He was a self-made man, someone who had struggled against social prejudices and poverty to become a success.

And he was successful—he ended up with a large house in Castleknock, an affluent suburb on the north side of Dublin, and he rapidly acquired the trappings of wealth; fancy cars and a boat on the Shannon. It was imprinted on our minds as kids how brilliant he was—he used to say that he had passed his exams in just two years when it had taken everyone else in his class three.

But it was only ever Da who told us how brilliant he was. I don't remember anyone else ever saying it. He was always telling me and my brothers that he was the most intelligent person we would ever meet, and I believed him.

Although I loved Da, I began to see a side to him at a very young age that wasn't nice. He never missed an opportunity to put people down. He was forever giving out about my Ma's parents; Nanny for smoking, Granddad for being half deaf and us kids for yelling at him all the time in case he couldn't hear us. His biggest gripe was the TV in Nanny and Granddad *O'Byrne's* house.

'It's always blaring 'cause your Granddad is deaf. Anyone with manners would turn it off when there are guests,' he'd moan.

Da considered himself a highly important guest when he visited anyone's home. He thought everyone should be delighted to see him and go out of their way to accommodate him.

As time passed, the more Da mixed with educated, successful people, the more obnoxious he became. It wasn't just his obnoxious behaviour that made me dislike him, though. It was his bedtime routine that I hated, and it goes back as far as I can remember.

*

Apparently, it's not true that all babies are beautiful because when I was born everyone said I looked like a plucked chicken with loose folds of skin. I was born in the bedroom of our house in Ballsbridge although I nearly arrived in the bathroom as the door got stuck while Ma was in there, and it was only that the midwife broke the door down that Ma made it into the bedroom in time, or so the story goes.

I was the first girl born to the family and I'm sure my Ma was delighted to have a little sister for my older brother, who was three years old by the time I arrived.

When I was three years old, Ma gave me and *Mark* a little baby brother called *Fergus*. The baby was a happy, placid baby and very easy to take care of.

My childhood memories start when I was about three. Some people might argue that you can't remember things that happened when you were that young, but I believe that you can. You may not remember whether it was winter or summer, whether you were in the hall or the sitting room, or even the exact details of the particular memory, but the emotions that go hand in hand with it are what you carry forward.

Memories of such times are very clear to me. I can remember certain events. And when the feelings are bad ones, they're even harder to forget.

I can't remember when exactly Da started calling to my room at night; all I do know for sure is that the bad feelings started when I was about three years old or a little older. I was very young when he started to abuse me. I can recall images of him, sneaking into my room.

He used to get into bed beside me and tell me stories about Granny as a little girl, and how she got lost in a fairy ring down the country and that she wasn't able to get out. He also told me stories about Granny going to school on a cow. I loved hearing the stories, but I didn't like when he would put his hands into my knickers and fondle my private area. As he talked, his fingers were constantly fiddling around my vagina, and it hurt me.

For a long time I thought it was normal for fathers to touch their daughters 'down there'; it was like a goodnight kiss or a hug. I'd been so damaged and my mind had become so warped that I remember thinking, how do other kids Da's do it to them, especially when there was more than one girl? It was such a normal part of my life.

The only difference between a goodnight kiss and what my Da did was that it didn't feel nice; it hurt and felt dirty. I figured that if you had to wash your hands every time you went to the bathroom, then there definitely was something dirty about 'down there'. That would also solve the question of why none of my friends spoke about their fathers touching them there. So I said nothing. That is how it started. While I was still a baby it started with him touching my private area and it progressed over the next few years, gradually getting worse and worse. When I look back now as an adult I can see that I had no choice in the matter;

we accept as normal the environment that parents create for us, and he created an environment of sexual abuse from the start. He groomed me as his victim from the beginning. I didn't have a hope.

*

In the very early days, I remember it being just Ma, the two boys and me most of the time. Da was home very little and when he was in a bad mood, a similar atmosphere swept through the house. Da earned the money and paid the bills while Ma cooked, cleaned and looked after all of us. In those days, everything was done by hand so housework was ten times harder than it is now. I'll never forget the day Da brought home the twin-tub and put an end to having to hand-wash the terry nappies in a bucket of water.

Da thought he was the best husband in the world when he presented Ma with such an advanced kitchen appliance. He was smiling so much I'm surprised his face didn't crack. From then on, all Da's presents had domestic themes. Now my Ma, like most women, was in favour of any household appliance that would make life easier for her, but when they were being given to her as gifts every birthday and Christmas, I think she wasn't too happy.

We moved from Ballsbridge to Fairview on the north side of Dublin when I was about three. That was in 1970. At the time, this was a move up in the world.

The new house was a three-bedroom semi-detached with a garage. It was a corner house. There were ten houses on either side of the street in this small cul de sac. At our end of the estate, there was a big wall surrounding an orchard. This was a place of wonderment to us kids. Over the years, most of us had a go at robbing apples from the canon and his housekeeper who lived there.

The Fairview house was very respectable. It had a good-sized front room, a sitting room and a small kitchen as far as I remember. Ma was delighted with it and glad to see the back of the old, damp redbrick in Ballsbridge.

I made my very first friends in that estate in Fairview. I was peering through the gates of my house, out on to the street and beyond, when a row of curious little faces came into my line of vision. They were all about the same age as me.

All were full of chatter and asked me all sorts of questions the way children do. They were fascinated by my blonde hair and blue eyes and kept poking their skinny arms through the grates in the gate to touch my hair and see if it not only looked different to their own brown hair but felt different too. These girls were to become the core of my primary school gang.

My clothes that first summer in Fairview consisted of teeny weenie shorts, skirts and dresses that only barely covered my knickers. It was an age of innocence that wouldn't last long. God when I think about it, my father must have loved it.

Fairview was a great place to grow up. I was at my happiest there, despite all that was going on behind closed doors. I loved my little friends. We were a close group. When you have a big bunch of kids growing up together there's bound to be some arguments from time to time, but if we fought one day, we were friends again the next. And there were always ways of wheedling your way back into your friends' favour. Like, if you were lucky enough to have a birthday party coming up you could hold it over the others by saying, 'If you don't play with me then you're not coming to my party tomorrow.' It was more a case of using your persuasive powers than being mean. But no matter what, we all went to each other's parties.

Our birthday parties were pretty simple back then. I don't remember getting expensive presents from my friends, actually I don't think we gave presents at all. The whole thrill of a party was that you became one year older and got to feast on all the sweets and fizzy drinks you could stomach. You were just so happy to be allowed play together and eat sugary treats. And whether you wanted it or not, you always got a slice of the birthday cake, wrapped in a napkin, to bring home with you.

Ma never let us down when it came to cakes and parties. The table would be crammed with popcorn, sponge cakes, fairy cakes and, my favourite treat of all, Rice Krispie buns. Even as an adult, it doesn't feel like a party to me until the Rice Krispie buns appear.

The all-important blowing out of the candles was the peak of excitement. Usually one of my brothers would sneak up behind me and blow the candles out with me which meant my wish wouldn't come true. So after some squabbling and Ma trying to pull us apart, the candles were relit and my brothers well warned.

Afterwards, we played all sorts of games like musical chairs or musical statues. They often ended in tears, though, with someone crying because they hadn't won or swearing blind that they hadn't moved when everyone knew they had.

Looking back, the summers seemed sunnier, warmer and longer when I was a child, but then it didn't matter too much what the weather was like, we still carried on with our games, inside or outside. We always called to each other's houses but I often waited for someone to call on me first. If it was raining outside, I enjoyed sitting on the couch, watching TV. But as soon as I got outside, it was hard to get me back in. I played all sorts of games with my friends: cycling, skipping, pushing our dolls' prams, What Time is it Mr Wolf? Red Rover Red Rover, rounders, hide-and-seek.

*

While I acted like a normal little girl, I wasn't one. I was always tense and, looking back on those days, I believe I was afraid. Even during the day, I never knew what lay around the corner. I remember going to Mass one Sunday with Da. Ma wasn't with us that day.

My body temperature raised and my face started burning when I saw him positioning himself, standing at the back of Fairview Church. Two younger girls were standing behind him. I saw him put his creepy hand behind his back and grope one of the children. I prayed she wouldn't say anything.

I didn't recognise her, and I thanked God for that, but I recognised that he seemed to have no fear. The little girl had a horrible experience in Mass that day.

I wasn't sure whether I felt worse watching him do it to another girl or when he did it to me. Doing it to me at least kept it hidden, but when he did it to someone else in front of me, I froze.

That was the first time I remember seeing Da touching anyone else besides me. At the time, I didn't understand why but I felt physically sick.

I didn't know if the little girl realised what was happening to her but I assumed she must have felt dirty, because I always did when he did that to me. My childish brain really couldn't make sense of this action. I thought it was something that daddies did with their little girls—not with other children.

I can recall seeing her face drain of colour. At the same time, mine was red and boiling. I couldn't wait to get out of the church. Ma always made us carry tissues up our sleeves, so on my way out, I took one and dipped it into the holy-water bowl. I dabbed my hot face with it, hoping that it might cool me down and also that it might wash away some of my shame and terror. Da just walked out of the church like nothing had happened. I think he must have enjoyed himself and that was all that mattered.

I remember being tired a lot after school. I would come home a lot of days, lie down on the couch and that was it, I'd sleep for the afternoon. This was a continuing habit of mine throughout my school years. I never got much sleep during the night and then during the day I couldn't stay awake. This was a symptom of my body clock being all over the place. Most kids would fall asleep shortly after being put to bed, but not me. I hated going to bed because I knew Da would soon follow.

In the beginning, I'd lie in bed waiting for him, my muscles rigid with tension. Then, as soon as the door opened, I'd relax every muscle in my body, not with relief, but so that he might think I was asleep and leave me alone. This was a useless exercise which never stopped Da. When he would finish, I'd come back to life and stay awake all night. How could I possibly go to sleep? My mind was contaminated with feelings of being dirty. I would lie awake for hours mulling dark thoughts over in my head.

I usually fell asleep in the early hours of the morning only to be awoken again shortly afterwards. I would be so exhausted the following day that I needed long naps to mentally recharge.

*

My earliest memories of school are from when I was six. I don't remember junior infants or senior infants too well, but I do remember first class in St Mary's National School in Fairview and have fond memories of my teacher Mrs Ray. She was exactly the type of teacher all kids love. She was very child-orientated and I don't ever remember her giving out to anyone. On their birthday, every student got a present. I distinctly remember the yellow, stretchy headband she gave me to keep my long blonde hair off my face. I kept that headband for years afterwards.

I had a great time in that school despite what was happening to me at home.

I managed to do all of my school work and I came to love reading and writing. I found maths pretty simple, so all in all, school was good. At the beginning of first class, I clung to Mrs Ray's every word and did whatever I could to please her. Any attention she gave me was like a ray of sunshine in my life. If she ticked my homework with a red pen, which meant 'very good', I was over the moon. But as the year went on her approval stopped being enough to keep me happy. I felt increasingly stressed and different to the other children. The feeling of emptiness intensified. I was depressed but at the age of six I had no understanding of what this even meant.

Even though I had lots of friends it didn't stop this feeling of dirtiness that often welled up inside. I was never sure how to describe it but I felt empty on the inside and blackened to the core. This feeling never left me. It was something that I felt every day of every waking hour. It was only in later years that I came to understand this feeling but at the time I didn't. It was just something that I learned to live with. It started to interfere with my feelings about school and I realised that school wasn't going to fill the void inside me. Because I wasn't sleeping much at night, I also was feeling very tired in class and I was unable to concentrate much.

It was a friend who discovered how easy it was to get out of class and this was the start of us going on the hop, or 'mitching' as we called it. It was also the beginning of the end of a normal life for me.

*

Bunking off school was my way of taking control and rebelling against what was happening, though at the time, I think I did it just because I could.

I never knew from week to week what day or time my friend would come knocking on Mrs Ray's classroom door. But once I heard the knock, I'd start packing. At first, I managed to get out once a week, then it was twice a week and before long I wasn't going in some days at all. Sometimes I got false notes from somewhere that said I was sick. It was too easy.

I used to hang around Main Street in Fairview instead. One of the side streets had rows of large three-story houses with big steps leading up to their doorways. If I was early enough I was able to steal the milk that had been left on their doorsteps. I never normally drank milk but this milk was different; because it was robbed it seemed somehow more precious and I used to gulp it down greedily. This became a daily thing and, just like the mitching, it was a great buzz.

I used to rob empty lemonade bottles from crates at the back of different shops so I could make some money. I would go into shops to sell the bottles back to the woman behind the counter. I think I got about 1p a bottle. I did this in a few different shops and when I'd gathered enough money I'd buy Fizzlesticks, Toffee Logs, Black Jacks and Fruit Salads. My favourite was the quarter mixes from the big clear jars with the black lids that had a mixture of Apple Sours, cough sweets and Bull's Eyes.

Before long, me and my accomplice had a great life going—lots of money, sweets and milk, and no school. Nobody paid too much attention to me mitching in those days. And if they did ask questions I had an excuse ready for them. One day we were sitting on a seesaw in Fairview Park when a woman came over.

'Have you no school kids?' she asked suspiciously.

I just said, 'No, Missus. There was a bomb scare.'

'Oh, okay.'

And off she went.

The Troubles were bad in the North around this time so there were a lot of bomb scares in Dublin. I remember going into town once with my aunt and my brother *Fergus*. We were walking along, minding our own business, when all of a sudden there was a loud noise and all around us people started dropping to the ground, face-down. A bomb had gone off nearby. I don't know which paramilitary group was behind it, all I know is that it went off pretty close to us and we were terrified. The three of us got home as fast as we could. So bomb scares were the norm back then and nobody ever batted an eyelid. So once I knew I was on to a good excuse, if anyone asked me, I'd tell them there'd been a bomb scare. This worked like a charm until one day a woman asked what school I was in.

'St Mary's,' I said.

She didn't say another word, just took off screaming, 'My babies! My babies!' at the top of her lungs.

Back in those days, schools could send you home for the day with no warning to the parents whatsoever. Whether you were four years old or ten, it didn't matter. Like if the heating was gone or a teacher was sick, we were all sent home.

Priests had the power to let you go early too. If they visited the school and you were able to answer your catechism questions correctly, they could say, 'Right, I'm going to tell the headmistress to let you off early today.' And he would. Could you imagine that happening today? With mothers at work—or even if they were at home. Young kids coming skipping home unannounced. Parents would go bloody mad. But back then no one seemed to mind.

The odd day mitching soon turned into the odd week and before long I was hardly in school at all. The inevitable happened and I eventually got caught because of something stupid. I came home with muck all over my shoes and there was no muck between my house and the school. My ma's instincts kicked into action.

One evening, I strolled in the front door as usual only to meet Ma in the hallway. I remember there was a full-length mirror in the hall so I could see both the front and the back of Ma at the one time. I now know that it's bad Feng Shui to have a mirror facing a doorway. I think it was probably more than a mirror that screwed up my life though.

As soon as my mother saw the muck on my shoes she began to question me.

'Where were you?' she asked.

'At school.'

'I know you're lying.'

Just then one of my friends came knocking on our door. Of all the girls to come knocking on the door at that exact moment, she was the girl that I didn't want to see. She couldn't lie to save her life. I was only six at the time but I still knew that you couldn't rely on her in this type of situation. But Ma was delighted to see her as she knew she'd definitely get the truth out of her.

'Was Audrey at school today?' Ma asked.

My friend looked scared. She knew I hadn't been in

school. She would never tell on you—she was loyal—but she just couldn't lie.

'Was Audrey in school today?' Ma repeated.

I nearly felt more sorry for her than I did for myself. She was in an awful position. The questioning went on for ages but my friend held her ground, refusing to answer 'yes' or 'no'.

She eventually whimpered that I hadn't been in school.

I went to run but Ma caught me. She never hit me but she told me to get changed into my pyjamas and wait until Da got home.

I was afraid of my da, but it was a different kind of fear than Ma thought. It wasn't the threat of a spanking that scared me. I knew Da was capable of much worse. All evening I listened out for the sound of Da's keys in the door. When the noise finally came I tried to fade into the shadows in the bedroom. But Da came storming in, his belt already off and wound around his balled-up fist. He told me to strip. He grabbed me and held me up by one arm, my two legs dangling mid-air, while he hit me with the belt; something he had never done before. It definitely hurt, but the scariest part of the whole thing was that as far as Da knew, I'd only been on the hop that one day. What would he have done to me if he'd found out it had actually been a couple of months?

I don't think the school ever told Ma and Da that I'd been out for so long. Going back was awful though. I had to hand Mrs Ray a note from my parents the following Monday morning. The letter was sealed and I had no idea what was written in it—I knew better than to read it. I know it was definitely Da and not me Ma that wrote it though.

My stomach was on fire and I was almost in tears handing the letter to Mrs Ray. She quietly read it.

'Okay Audrey, you can sit down,' she said in a disappointed tone of voice. She didn't give out to me or pass any comment whatsoever. I felt so bad for letting her down. She was so nice and I didn't like her thinking I was bold.

Getting caught didn't stop me from continuing to mitch from school. To me, mitching was my way of coping with my da. It was a way of rebelling but when I think back, I was probably crying out for help. The problem was that no one could hear me.

Chapter Two

In the midst of the abuse I suffered, I tried to act like a normal child.

I played with dolls, wore bright colours and played with other little girls but inside I was falling apart.

That indescribable feeling of being dirty was never far from my mind. It consumed me.

It is hard to explain the impact that sexual abuse has on a six-year-old girl. In my case, it distorted my whole life in ways that I am only now beginning to understand. Though I knew instinctively that what was happening to me at the time was wrong, I didn't know why it was wrong.

I had been brought up to believe that Da was right in everything he said and did, so I believed he was doing nothing wrong. In fact, I blamed myself for feeling bad about his nightly visits, which I assumed to be only natural. I guess I believed it was my reaction to him that was unnatural. To cope, I tried to live what I thought to be a normal childhood.

The tragedy is that anyone who would have known me at the time probably thought I was that normal child, as that is what I pretended to be.

The abuse was my secret; one which I shared with Da alone.

I acted like a normal little girl because I wanted to be one. I think this is why no one noticed what was happening. I acted like other children. The tell-tale signs only became apparent later in my life. At that time, I was an ordinary girl who did what other children did but I was fearful of my father. I wasn't scared of him being violent, I was scared of the power that he held over me.

This manifested itself in all sorts of strange ways. On Saturdays, which was my favourite day because I usually spent most of it in my pyjamas watching all my favourite television programmes, I would get up early and tiptoe by Ma and Da's bedroom.

I would head downstairs and lay newspapers on the ground before pouring out cereal. Ma thought I was being good doing this but it was really because I was afraid of Da. If I had spilled cereal on the sitting-room floor, he would have stopped me watching my favourite programmes.

So I'd set bowls of cereal down in front of the box and tune in to all my top shows like *Daktari*, *Swap Shop* and *Riverside Tales* among many others. I loved these programmes because they were alternate worlds into which I could escape.

But to the outside world, Da seemed like the best father a child could wish for.

Our family spent more weekends away on holiday than at home and we had a car when our neighbours were still riding bicycles.

We even had a colour television and access to cable channels long before our neighbours had them. In fact, I can still remember the day we got cable television.

Back in those days, RTÉ did not start transmitting until 3p.m. in the afternoon.

If you switched on the television, all you saw was a giant clock counting down the time till the programmes started.

One day, when I arrived home from school, I saw Ma perched in front of the television. I knew it was a few minutes to 3p.m. so I thought she was just watching the countdown.

It took me a minute or two to register that she was actually pressing other buttons on the TV and that we had new stations.

I couldn't believe it.

Now I could watch *Little House on the Prairie*, *The Waltons*, *The Brady Bunch*, *Magpie*, *Rainbow* and *Sesame Street*. As far as I was concerned, the new stations were the best thing to ever happen to me.

I had hours and hours of pure escapism at my fingertips. A colour television set arrived soon after. I can remember its arrival as if it happened yesterday.

Ma called us in for tea one evening. Once we were all seated at the table, I heard Da bustling about in the hall, making a racket. Suddenly, he peered around the corner, a huge cardboard box in his hands.

'Bring your tea into the sitting room, I have a surprise for you,' he said.

We were never allowed to eat in the sitting room so we knew Da had to have something to show us.

When his audience were all assembled, Da unveiled his

surprise and sat back like a proud magician awaiting the gasps of surprise.

There, sitting before us, was a big colour television set. Da plugged it in and began tuning the channels as we waited excitedly.

His timing couldn't have been more perfect 'cause there was a programme on about the Bay City Rollers. How much more colourful could you get?

Although Da hated TV, that night he sat down and watched it without complaining for once in his life.

He may not have liked television very much but that night he loved being the centre of attention of us kids. And we loved doting on him.

It is memories like these that most confuse and upset me. If Da hadn't been a child abuser, would he have been the best father in the world?

Maybe. I don't know because I can't think of him being anything other than an abuser.

When I was a child I wanted him to be the best father. This partly explains why I blamed myself for what he did to me and why I remained silent for years. I didn't want to say anything because he was my father, the man who brought me into this world, the man who provided for me, the man who was supposed to protect me.

Then I think back and remember and I am confronted by the truth.

He was not a role model but someone who pretended to love me so he could sexually abuse me.

This was the true side to his character; the one that only some little girls saw.

*

Da was a predatory child abuser. He abused me whenever he could and never missed an opportunity to destroy my childhood. When I think back to those days, the memories of what happened to me are as clear in my memory as if they happened yesterday.

He gratified himself sexually no matter what the risk or the cost to me.

Anyone who isn't familiar with the activities of child abusers often find it hard to comprehend how children are abused or what that involves. Child abuse has become a word that is bandied about without anyone giving much consideration to what it involves. There are different types of paedophiles and abusers, and Da was one of the worst kinds. He spent his time grooming young girls, until it got to the point where many of his victims—like me—couldn't even pinpoint exactly when the abuse started.

He was so clever about how he would groom a victim. It might start with a game of tickles, where he would chase a girl and tickle her. In my case, when I was comfortable with him tickling me on my hips, he would gradually move his hands down, until he was 'tickling' me under my knickers, between my legs. This was a process that didn't happen overnight, and it was this behaviour that made it so dangerous, because he made it seem so normal.

He also took every possible opportunity to meet other little girls. Da, I would learn in later years, was also an opportunistic paedophile and would sexually interfere with a child when he saw an opportunity.

I can recall specific events, which now chill me to the bone. One day I went out with Da on a message. He was driving along in the rain when he suddenly stopped to pick up a lady and a couple of children who were complete strangers to us. He asked her where she lived and told them to get in out of the rain, that he would drop them home.

Obviously having me in the car gave the impression that he was a family man and could be trusted. The woman said she was very grateful, and rushed her girls into the back of the car. Da told me to move into the middle so the girls could sit at the window seats and look out. I did what I was told without thinking about it too much. One of the girls, who was around nine years old sat behind Da's seat and started drawing little pictures on the window pane in the condensation. As the woman shook herself dry and organised her belongings, she told Da how kind he was.

'I was a bit wary of getting in the car with you, but then I saw your lovely little blonde daughter.'

'That's my Audrey, my only little girl,' he replied smoothly and as he spoke, with the car still stationary, the little girl who was on my right suddenly stopped drawing and froze. My da's hand had stretched in between the doors of the car and his seat into the back, and up the little girl's skirt. He continued chatting to the lady while his dirty hand was up her daughter's skirt. The knots in my stomach were so tight I couldn't straighten myself up. When we finally got to their house, Da and the lady were all smiles and thank you's. The other little girl just gave me a filthy look, scrunching her face as if what had just happened to her was all my fault. I felt that it was.

There were lots of other opportunities for Da. Most Friday nights, we would go to swimming baths in Artane. I didn't go to swimming lessons. I would just copy people, and stay up somehow. That's if some older kid wasn't holding you down till you couldn't breathe, which was a popular game then. Swimming was brilliant, except when my da came. I had the feeling that he was touching girls that I didn't know in the pool and I was dead embarrassed.

I could see what he was doing because he had been doing it to me for as long as I could remember. His roaming hands, touching where he was not supposed to touch. I hated his hands. Yet he did it in such a way that you weren't marked; there were no scars, no pain at that stage and age.

Although he was abusing me, I seemingly had nothing to give out about because the bruises were all inside. That's how I knew what he was doing, and how it felt for them, those other girls. I could see where his hands were and the games he played. His hands, I hated his hands, they were always where they shouldn't be.

But what could I say when I was so young. I couldn't say 'he hurt me' because at that stage he was using his grotesque hands to rub me down there, gently grooming me, bit by bit, going further and further each time. There was nothing obvious to tell at the beginning except I felt dirty, confused. I was told, of course, to keep away from strangers because they would hurt you. My da was not a stranger, nor was I cut or bleeding. It was hard to say that he had attacked me in any shape or form.

*

Another way Da made his behaviour appear normal was through his behaviour with me around other people. I was not just abused at home but even on holiday when I was surrounded by adults.

A holiday we spent on a farm was one such incident that I remember well.

My emotions still do somersaults and my stomach contracts when I think about this holiday.

The good and the bad memories wash over me and it's hard to separate them because they go hand in hand. It's a vicious circle. Once you recall good memories from a particular event, the bad ones come too, nipping at their heels. And the bad ones only end up soiling the good ones. It has taken me years but I can now distil them a little better.

I remember the farmhouse holiday for two reasons. Firstly, 'cause I got to spend a lot of time with Granddad and Nanny Delaney and I have fond memories of that. I remember Nanny in particular from this holiday. She used to bring us out to a field near the farmhouse that had cattle in it.

Jesus, they'd be running at her left, right and centre, and she'd be running right back—she was very brave. But she didn't go to the field to taunt the animals. She wanted to gather mushrooms before they were trodden on by the animals.

We wouldn't dare step into the field with her though 'cause we were terrified of the cattle. So she'd pick the mushrooms all by herself. I don't remember what we did with them afterwards—whether Ma cooked them or what—but I've loved mushrooms ever since. They always remind me of how brave Nanny was.

The second reason I remember that holiday is on account of the abuse I was forced to endure and all the insecurities and unnatural feelings that were left swarming around in my head all the time.

I made some new friends during the holiday, and we all palled around together on the farm. But as usual Da made sure to befriend my new playmates, and he was constantly hanging around with us kids. One of the girls was having a birthday party during the holiday and we were all invited— having a party while on holiday was a double celebration. Da was hanging around with us one day when I noticed he had disappeared off with one of the girls. I got the familiar sick feeling in my stomach that I always got when I knew something horrible was going to happen.

The next day, the little girl who was having the party marched up to me, flanked on either side by all the other girls.

'You're not invited to my party,' she said, glaring at me, and she marched off. It was so obvious to me that someone had told her about my da. All the other girls were invited, except me. I had done nothing, yet that overwhelming feeling of being dirty and disgusting washed over me. I felt like a piece of scum. I didn't know why I was so bad and so different.

I didn't tell Ma that I wasn't invited, because I was so ashamed. Instead, I stood outside the house on the day of the party, hoping the girls would take pity on me and invite me in. But they didn't. I was all by myself, sobbing uncontrollably. But no tears were falling. It was all on the inside. I had this awful pain that I couldn't shake. I was only a child and the weight of the world was on my shoulders.

I had started to get growing pains. I can't remember much of that holiday because I have buried the memories deep in my subconscious but I do remember one particular night when I woke up with a terrible throbbing sensation in my legs. The pains were quite severe.

On that holiday, Nanny and Granddad Delaney had their own room in that cottage but Ma, Da, the boys and me were all in the one room.

One night, I was moaning about my leg during the night and eventually I decided to sleep elsewhere to help me relax.

I dragged a blanket out with me and made a bed on the sofa. I had only just lay down on it when I heard the door creaking open behind me and in walked Da, wearing nothing but a pair of Y-fronts. Muttering something about wanting to see if I was all right, he came over and took my pyjamas and knickers off roughly.

'I'm giving your feet a rub to help your sore legs,' he said, peeling off his Y-fronts as he drew me towards him. He started rubbing himself in between my two feet, up and down, over and over. Several minutes later he came to a finish, pulled up his underpants and stumbled blindly back to his bed.

The strange thing is that I don't remember there ever being a mess when he would masturbate against me. I don't remember him ejaculating, but maybe he did and I've blocked it out. It's hard to know, but one thing I do know for sure is that he got some sort of self-gratification out of this behaviour. Whether he ejaculated or not, he made sure that he enjoyed it. When he finished, he left me there to dress myself again.

I have never forgotten what happened that night. I was beginning to understand at this point that my da was only using me for his own pleasure. He didn't come out to rub my legs because they were sore—that much I was able to comprehend. Whatever he was doing with me, it was all about him. With this newfound realisation, I dressed myself with tears streaming down my face, the pain in my legs being the physical part matching the pain in my heart.

When he woke the next morning, he went about his business as if nothing had happened. Whereas I had been enjoying the holiday up to the previous day, I now felt myself slipping into the familiar black hole as I realised that I wasn't safe from Da no matter where we were. It wouldn't matter how many adults were surrounding me—he would still do exactly as he pleased with me. If he couldn't physically get at me, I knew he would find some other innocent girl to molest. He was insatiable. I spent the rest of the holiday in a state of numbness, making sure that I slept in the company of others for the remainder of the holiday.

*

When I was seven, Ma told me that we were going to be getting a new baby. The boys and myself were sent to stay with Nanny and Granddad.

I can still remember the smell of coddle cooking as I stood in the kitchen waiting for the call to tell us that the new baby had arrived.

Oh, I so hoped it would be another boy. Everyone thought that with two brothers already, a little girl would want a sister. I think some people secretly thought I was just jealous and wanted to remain the only girl in the family. I couldn't explain it myself at the time but I had this dark cloud hanging over me.

I feared for the baby if it was a girl. It would mean trouble. No, no, the baby had to be a boy. Everyone else kept saying that the gender didn't matter so long as the child was healthy.

But the health of the new tot never even crossed my mind. All I cared about was that it was a boy, and if it wasn't then I wanted to die. I couldn't take it any longer. I was only seven yet there I was, my stomach in knots and me barely able to eat from the anxiety of waiting for that call.

They all thought I couldn't settle down 'cause I missed Ma but I was very at home in that house. I loved it there. It was safe and full of people who loved me. And I didn't spend the night-time lying awake, watching and waiting. I slept right through. I would have stayed there forever if I'd been allowed.

A real fire always burned in that house. You could just sit at it for hours soaking up the heat, while the adults jokingly warned you that if you sat with your back to the fire for too long you'd get a cold in your kidneys.

I was sitting in front of the fire in the sitting room one cold November evening when the phone call finally came.

My aunt came in and told us the baby was a large, chubby boy. He was a real heavyweight for those days seemingly. Ma and Da had named him *Dan*.

'Oh, God. Thank you,' was all I could think.

'It's a boy! It's a boy!' I cried over and over as I danced around the room.

Nobody in the house knew the significance of the baby being a boy. It took the responsibility off my shoulders. I could breathe again. The thunderous black cloud overhead disappeared but little did I know at the time that it wouldn't stay away for long.

Now I had two little baby brothers and I planned on being their second Mammy. I would tell them stories and play with them. Anything to keep them with me and safe at night. Once I was sure they were asleep and their door was shut, I would sooner make up an excuse to call Da into my room if it meant he would leave them alone. Better me than them I thought. On some level, I was already aware that Da was interested in girls and not boys. I knew that Da didn't 'tickle' the boys. He never went near my brothers, yet he always wanted to tickle girls, but I was too young to be sure so it was a case of better safe than sorry.

A few days later Ma arrived home from hospital with the newest addition to the family. We were all bundled into the car for the drive home to Fairview.

Mammy sat in the front passenger seat and me and the boys sat on the edge of the back seat, with baby *Dan* lying behind us in a carrycot. It took up the whole of the back seat. He had certainly claimed his place in the family, literally edging me and my brothers out of the way, but none of us minded. He was so cute that I couldn't take my eyes off him.

Whether Mammy was in the mood or not, all the neighbours flocked to see the new baby. *Dan* was such a cuddly child, with gorgeous big, puffy cheeks and huge dimples, that he earned himself the name Puddens. He was never fat; all *Dan*'s chubbiness was in his jolly little face. I thought both *Fergus* and *Dan*, my two baby brothers, were equally gorgeous. The older one with his huge saucer-like blue eyes, long eyelashes and placid, happy-go-lucky nature. And then the new baby, with his big smile and endearing dimples. God, love didn't get any better than what I felt for these two.

As time went on, I fell even more in love with Puddens. I used to make him pretend to be a baby monkey and tell him that I was the Mammy monkey and if he clung to me I'd carry him along. He'd wrap his tiny little arms around my neck and his legs around my waist and off we'd go.

I was very close to my other younger brother *Fergus* too. We played together a lot, talked loads and just got on well without any fighting.

You couldn't fight with him anyway even if you'd wanted to—it just wasn't in his nature. And all he had to do was bat his big Bambi eyes at you and your heart would melt.

We did everything together as a family back then. We certainly earned ourselves the Brady Bunch title, which some of my friends had bestowed on us.

Chapter Three

When I look back on my childhood, I can see why people thought that I was a happy and content child. I am sure that most people who knew me probably believed that I was happier than most youngsters.

I liked games, playing dolls and other children's activities but dancing and performing were my favourites.

I joined the Billie Barry School of Dance when I was about eight years old. I learned tap dancing at the school and I loved it. I loved the noise and the exhilarating sound of it.

It became the event in my week. It was something pure and wholesome; it was innocent fun and it was something that Da hadn't tainted, so I could enjoy it in a relaxed atmosphere. I should have known he would take away this last remnant of innocence from me sooner or later.

Every Saturday at 3p.m. I went to the Carlton Hall in Marino on the north side of Dublin and learned how to tap dance.

I went there with my cousin *Kate*, who was my best friend. My little brother *Fergus* started as well, and he was really good. He and I always palled around together and if I started something he was quick to follow, not only because he wanted to be with me but because we liked similar things.

There was only one thing that I hated about dancing and that was the uniform we had to wear. It was a white polo-neck, a short red swing skirt and tap shoes. The boys were lucky because they didn't have to wear a uniform. I loved the tap shoes though, especially the noise they made on the floor as you tapped along to the rhythm of the music. The first pair of tap shoes you got—the junior ones—were always white and you had to scuff coat them every now and then when the leather became worn.

My attitude to dance shoes changed when I got my first pair of black tap shoes. I'd say me and *Kate* wore out the lino on the floors in both our houses.

Tap shoes, or black tap shoes to be precise, looked fabulous. As far as I was concerned they were the height of sophistication.

The dance classes cost about 50p each. An old woman, who everyone called Aul Aunty Something, collected the money before the class and ticked off your name to show that you'd paid. She looked old to me, probably about 90, so it didn't take us long to realise that she was a bit doddery. So we would pretend to put our money in a biscuit tin she used to use; we'd rattle it around a bit so it sounded like the money had dropped in and then Aul Aunty Something would tick our names off the list. We'd spend the 50p on sweets in the little tuck shop they had at the back of the hall. We never thought we were doing anything wrong. We had no real value on money; we just loved the buzz of keeping the 50p. And we loved our sweets too. I would never have dared to take somebody else's 50p out of the tin, or keep my own 50p and just not bother going dancing.

Tap dancing was an escape for me. I knew I was good at it and, for a little while at least, I could forget my troubles.

*

I hadn't been dancing long when I was asked to attend an audition for a commercial on RTÉ. The auditions were to be held in a studio that Billie Barry had built at the back of her garden and Billie herself would be picking the children she thought were good enough to proceed to the next round.

A lot of the kids had been in the club for yonks and were really good, so when I got picked to audition I was thrilled.

I wore a red-and-white striped catsuit to the audition. I thought it looked really cool. But on my way there, I wore a jacket that covered the top part of the suit, so it looked like I was just wearing red and white trousers, which, on their own, didn't look nearly as cool. I was teased all the way to the audition, with other kids laughing at me and saying I looked square.

My confidence was shattered by the time I arrived at Billie Barry's house. I would go as far as to say that I was convinced that I had worn the wrong outfit and now looked stupid, so I struggled through the audition.

When I was called back a week later for another audition, I thought it was a mistake. This time, I was told to bring two sets of clothes with me and both had to be Irish made. Ma was always very supportive of my desire to dance, and she was proud as punch when I got the call back. She made sure that I had all the outfits I needed, and we both headed off for the audition. This time round my confidence was high and my heart was fully in it. I did the audition and a few weeks later Ma got a call telling her I'd got the job. Myself and a good few other kids would be singing a song about chicken. The song went like this:

You can do a lot with chicken.
Chicken in a sanger.
You can do a lot with chicken.
Chicken Maryland.
You can put it in a stew.
It's full of goodness too.
You can do a lot, do a lot, do a lot with chicken.

I only appeared on screen for a few seconds but getting picked was still a great feeling of accomplishment. I think I got paid about £60 for it too if I remember correctly. Plus, I got to go to RTÉ and I was excited about what stars I'd get to meet there. I had my heart set on seeing Mr Spring and Mr Sprong. They were cartoon characters from an advert for the biscuits Jacobs Kimberley Mikado and Coconut Creams. I obviously didn't get to see them but I still got to feel like a mini celebrity for the day.

Dancing and singing allowed me to hide the dirt inside me from the outside world, or so I believed. This was the only explanation for why the people from RTÉ had hired me for the advertisement. Obviously they couldn't see the real me, otherwise they'd never have put me on telly. When I was singing and dancing, an invisible barrier surrounded me and allowed me to hide the real me. It was a great feeling. I could disguise myself and, for a short while, I could pretend I was clean and normal, just like everyone else.

*

Dancing was a form of escapism which distracted me from my secret life, which at times threatened to consume me.

Da was continuing to visit my room at night in order to abuse me. I would lie in bed, rigid with fear wondering if he would leave me alone. I was so afraid to fall asleep, as believe it or not, I felt I would be more vulnerable if I was asleep. Because he worked in an office, his hands were smooth and soft, but compared to those of an eight-year-old's, they were huge. His large fingers would probe my vagina roughly, and he would thrust them into me as he rubbed his erection against my back, breathing heavily in my ear. My body was so tense and tight that I couldn't help but gasp with pain as he roughly grabbed me, but I quickly learned to zone out of my physical situation by a variety of different means.

By this stage, I had learned to pretend to be asleep and try to clear my head of all thoughts except for those about dancing.

At other times, I'd pick away at the wallpaper on my

bedroom wall, slowly peeling it away in miniature strips, as he abused me.

It was a simple form of distraction. I would have done anything to distract my mind from the monster my father had become.

But, of course, peeling the wall paper also got me into trouble.

I had come to look on my bedroom not as a place of sanctuary but as a place of torture.

I didn't care what it looked like and was content to leave it untidy with clothes and toys left strewn all over the floor. I would go so far as to say that walking through it was like walking through a minefield. Ma was always asking me to keep it clean. But I hated the fucking place. Why would I want to keep my room tidy when I despised it? I didn't want to spend time there. It was a dirty place in my eyes anyway—with or without all the junk littering it. I associated it with depravation and humiliation.

I did what I could to make it a safe place for me.

When Puddens was born, I used to drag his cot from the boys' room into mine, so I could go to sleep with him beside me.

It gave me a lovely warm feeling inside having him nearby. I was always very maternal. Da always moved his cot back to the boys' room though. I don't know why he did this when I clearly liked having him there. With Puddens beside me, I didn't feel lonely anymore.

I always lay on my left side at night, facing the wall, so that when I needed to escape things I could just reach over and start picking at the wallpaper.

I couldn't stop my father from abusing my body but even as a young girl I managed to escape mentally by not looking at what he did—it was a way of travelling to a different world.

I didn't take in any of the noises or things that happened to me. In many ways, peeling away the wallpaper was my private drug.

I can recall lying there as Da abused me and discovering that our house had clearly been owned by loads of families before us 'cause underneath my floral layer of wallpaper there were old layers and patterns that fascinated me. I liked imagining the different families and the different rooms that matched each layer. I'd use the patterns to make up stories in my head—the flowery pattern, the stripey one; they all had a different story. With each layer, I was uncovering a different life, and the best part was that it wasn't my life so I could make it as nice and adventurous as I liked.

But every morning, more and more bits of discarded wallpaper would be scattered all over my bed like flecks of confetti, until eventually there was a big, circular bare patch left on the wall. As obvious as it was that I was responsible for it, I denied it to Ma. I swore blind it wasn't me. I knew she knew it was me and she knew that I knew but I still wouldn't admit it. Looking back, I was just daring her to catch me doing it; I was practically begging her.

I now believe that I was trying to force Ma to come into my bedroom to catch Da.

Peeling the wallpaper was my way of saying, 'Why don't you look in on me at night, Ma? You know I'm up to no good in here, peeling the wallpaper away. Catch me. See who's in here with me. Take the time. Come on in and see what I'm doing.'

I'm not sure if I really wanted her to catch Da with me though. In fact, I know I didn't. I knew her heart would have been broken. I wasn't sure if I could handle that.

I didn't want to break up our family. I knew there was something wrong with Da though I wasn't exactly sure what it was.

More than anything, I didn't want Ma to be hurt. I loved her so much, I wanted to protect her. I was also frightened of what might happen. So I just continued peeling away the wallpaper and dancing.

*

Coming up to Christmas during my second year in the school, Billie Barry held more auditions for the Christmas pantomime in the Gaiety. Only the very best would make the grade. There were hundreds of kids auditioning and each one seemed even better than the last. The actress and singer Maureen Potter was in the panto. I thought she was great, so performing with her would be a dream come true.

Ma had been bringing me and my brothers to pantomimes since we were tiny so I knew what a big deal it was and how good you had to be. They were choosing kids for both the main roles and for understudies in case the main kids ever got sick. I'd have been over the moon to be picked as an understudy and to get to the stage for even just one night out of the whole run. I'd have sacrificed anything for the chance. I even swore I'd go to Mass. For a long time now, I'd been getting away with not going. On Sunday mornings Ma would go up to Fairview church and get Mass out of the way early so that she could spend the afternoon baking and cooking for the big roast dinner. We were all told to go when we got up but I usually either played sick or just wandered up the lane for an hour and then came back. I hated Mass but for a chance to be an understudy in the pantomime, I was prepared to do anything.

The auditions finally arrived and, like the ones for RTÉ, they narrowed us down to a small group of hopefuls. Then they called out our names. I'll never forget it. A big group of us were standing in the middle of the hall, all practically biting our fingernails down to the cuticles with the nerves. I thought I was hearing things when they called my name out. I was going to be in the Gaiety with Maureen Potter and I was part of the team, not just an understudy. My brother *Fergus* was picked as well but because of his age he had to share the role with another little lad. But it was doubly exciting that the two of us had gotten through. I couldn't stop hugging and kissing him and his big blue eyes got even bigger because I was squeezing him so tightly. I'd even managed to get away with my promise to God that I'd go back to Mass 'cause I'd sworn I'd go back only if I got to be an understudy; I had made the full team so that was different.

Making the full team also meant extra classes. You did your normal tap classes with Billie Barry and then you were sent for extra training in the hall next door where Billie Barry's daughter Lorraine taught modern dancing. Now, this style of dance was much cooler. I was in my element and what made it even sweeter was that the classes were free. The rehearsals for the Gaiety were then separate to the modern-dance classes so I was spending loads of time every week doing the thing I loved.

Alongside Maureen Potter, the rest of the cast seemed lovely. All the girls were head over heels in love with this new, up-and-coming singer called Johnny Logan, who later went on to win the Eurovision for Ireland. They thought he was gorgeous. I barely noticed him though because I had a crush on Jonathan Ryan, the guy who played my father on stage. There was just something really lovely about him.

*

When the panto kicked off, we were on stage every night of the week and twice on Saturdays and Sundays. Even as the weeks went by and I got used to the routine, I still realised how lucky I was to be there and I never once took it for granted. It went on from October to just past Easter and I didn't miss one show. The reason I remember it going on until Easter is because Maureen threw a big Easter party for the kids at the end of the run and she even bought us all eggs.

It was a fabulous few months. The kids were only on stage for the first half of the show, and after that it was just the adults. I'd have loved to have stayed for the whole thing but there were laws about how long children were allowed work for. I could see why they needed understudies, though, because some of the kids ran out of energy as the shows went on, or got sick, so there was always a bit of swapping going on. I didn't want to miss a moment of the glory and fun but there was one particular night when I really thought I had blown it for myself.

I was on stage one night during a love song—I think it was 'The First Time I Ever Saw Your Face'. Johnny Logan started singing and myself and another girl in the panto had to sit at his feet, looking up at him and listening attentively. It was the only song that we didn't have to dance to. We just had to sit still and do nothing. Now it wasn't that I didn't like Johnny—I did—but I could be a bit of a devil at times. I don't know what got into me this one night but I just couldn't help myself. Johnny was wearing a pair of knee-length panto-style trousers and it was too tempting not to start plucking at the hairs on his legs. I knew I was hurting him and that he was struggling to sing but here I was in the Gaiety, with the spotlight on me, and poor Johnny at my mercy. It was too much of a high to pass up on. So I just kept plucking away at the hairs on his legs. The girl sitting the other side of him saw me and started giggling as she started on his other leg. It was the funniest thing ever. The conductor in the orchestra pit saw what we were at and started narrowing his eyes at us, so we calmed down a bit but by then the song was nearly over.

I knew I was in big trouble.

At half time I was waiting for them to kick me out of the show altogether. But nobody said a word to me so I was kept in stomach-knotting suspense until the following night. The wait was terrible. I don't remember who gave out to me. It wasn't Johnny anyway. It could have been our choreographer. But I got a stern warning and reprimanded something awful. They let us stay in the end though. They had plenty of kids to fill my space so they could easily have kicked me out. I was so happy and relieved.

You might ask why I engaged in such behaviour. The truth is that I did it to attract attention. The abuse at my father's hands was now an almost nightly occurrence. My actions were all aimed at drawing attention to myself in the hope that someone would rescue me. It was my way of screaming for help without raising my voice. I was no longer a child because he had stolen my childhood.

*

The very last night of the pantomime was heartbreaking. My co-stars had become like a family to me over those few months. I can remember buying goodbye presents to give to Maureen and Jonathan. I bought Maureen a cheap little ornament. I was a little shy about giving it to her so I waited until she was alone before going up to her.

'Here Aunt Maureen, I got you a goodbye present,' I said.

Her eyes widened and she oooh'ed and aaah'ed as if I was giving her a piece of treasure that she'd been searching for her whole life.

'That's absolutely beautiful. I am so delighted. Aren't you very clever picking up something I've been wanting for ages,' she said.

'It was only cheap and it should have been in a pair. But I only had money for one,' I explained.

'Ah, but I have the other one at home and now I can put the two of them together. Thanks so much.'

She was a nice woman. She had that old-fashioned way about her that was sincere. I have nothing but fond memories of her. There were times that I wished she was part of our family. When you are a child you believe that some adults can solve your problems. I know now they can't but when I was a child I still believed in the goodness of people.

The other person I bought a present for was Jonathan— the man who played my father on stage. He was just so nice to me and I guess, for a while, he filled this little hole I had in my heart. I bought him a fake-leather belt. It was only when he went to put the belt on that I realised I'd gotten him a kids' belt.

'Sure can't I pierce a hole at the tip of the belt,' he said laughing. 'I am going to wear it every day from now on.'

As the hours ticked by that night I got more and more upset at the thought of it all coming to an end. Several years' worth of sadness swelled up inside of me. It was one of the saddest nights of my life and I don't think anyone understood how I felt. The cast had been my family for the last few months; Jonathan was my stage da, Maureen my stage aunt, and the rest of the cast were like brothers and sisters. When we were on stage nothing bad could happen. The singing and dancing was like a magical spell that transformed me into a good, clean person. Every night, hundreds of people watched me, with the spotlight shining down on me, and every night they applauded me—no one ever saw my dirty soul. The magic worked. All they saw was the singing, dancing, smiling me. Not the real me, the worthless, empty, no-good me whose Da did what he did because she let him.

At the end of the show, as the crowd were applauding us, Jonathan picked me up and spun me around. He was wearing the belt on stage and I was thrilled. I put my arms around his neck, not wanting to ever let go of him.

'I'm going to miss you so much,' I cried, clinging on to him tightly and soaking his shirt with my tears.

'I'll miss you too, don't forget that. Sure didn't I wear the belt and all for this special occasion?'

I was crying so hard my throat hurt but I welcomed the pain as some sort of relief. I just didn't want the night to end.

*

I continued to dance for another year or so until shortly after we moved house again, this time to Castleknock. I was in the car with Da one Saturday when I decided never to go back to the classes again.

Da was giving another little girl and her mother a lift to a class and he made some comment about what a beautiful child the girl was and that he'd be free to take her to classes.

I froze when he said those words. I knew what he wanted and I wasn't going to let him have it.

I was not going to let him break into that world. It was something I had for myself; something that he couldn't pollute.

I never went back to the Billie Barry School after that. I wanted to keep it as something he hadn't touched—something happy and pure. And so I stopped dancing.

Chapter Four

In 1979, my family moved from Fairview in north Dublin because Da said he wanted to live in a more upmarket community. We moved to Castleknock, which is an affluent part of Dublin and lies close to the Phoenix Park.

I remember the day when I first saw the house he bought and thinking it was a mansion. It had lots of bedrooms, a big kitchen and a games room, and was situated in the centre of Castleknock village. It oozed of money. You might say it had 'I'm successful and rich' stamped all over it.

The house move was a turning point in both his and my life for a number of reasons. I didn't want to leave Fairview. I loved my friends there, and I loved the area. I hated moving to Castleknock but a part of me believed that the new house would bring with it a new hope, and that Da would stop coming into me. I wasn't to know that Da had other ideas. At that point I associated my home in Fairview with the horrors of sexual abuse and bodily degradation. It was a place where my childhood had been stolen by a father who plundered my body. I hated the bedroom where my father visited me at night to abuse me. I hated the furniture, the carpets and the wallpaper in my bedroom. It was for this reason that I never bothered to keep my bedroom tidy. It was always in a state. I never cared about keeping it clean because it was always a sordid, dirty, horrible room to me anyway. I preferred to keep it dirty, because that was the way I felt about it.

On the other hand, I didn't want to leave my friends and to leave behind everything I knew.

It was from this point onwards that I began to be consumed by an overwhelming sense of insecurity and low self-esteem. I also suffered from severe anxiety.

I never spoke to anyone about it until years later but the ongoing abuse affected every aspect of my life.

I wondered whether my family would be torn apart if Da was caught. These feelings consumed and haunted me. I was afraid that if I told anyone, my family and I would be separated. This was a very big fear of mine and it coloured my behaviour.

I kept my mouth shut throughout this time because I was too young to understand that it wasn't my fault at all. I decided to just put up with it and do the best I could at not letting anyone find out. As far as I was concerned, it was my fault. There was something about me that made him do it; something dirty and he could see that filth in me. I didn't want to hurt everyone just so I could feel better.

I loved my ma and brothers so much, and I pictured us all going into different homes and being taken away. I couldn't face the prospect of not living with my brothers and Ma. She didn't have a job, and I worried about how she would cope. She'd be crying all the time and I felt that it would all be my fault, so in my childish brain I concluded it was better for everyone if I said nothing.

*

Da used the move to Castleknock to further improve his credibility. In many respects, the move represented the completion of his transformation into a new man.

My father spent his life trying to forget his past, conceal his depravations and trying to act out the role of a self-made man. He was always too ashamed to tell anyone he'd been born on Gardiner Street; that he came from humble beginnings, which I think would have shown that he was even more talented.

The house in Castleknock was his new start in life and his castle. And he wanted to show his own family what a great man he was. I don't believe he saw anything wrong with his sexual interest in children.

He was a man who constantly referred to his own achievements, boasted about his business acumen and spoke to others as if they were beneath him. He had an opinion on everything. I listened to him talk about subjects that he knew nothing of, and wondered how anyone could tolerate him.

The unemployed were one of his favourite targets. He would often say that people who claimed the dole were living off the state and should be made work. He would offer his opinions on everything, regardless of whether anyone wanted to hear them or not.

I think he felt compelled to exaggerate his own importance in order to conceal his weakness.

It was only in later years that I really came to understand that my father was an illusionist and a manipulator. Every breath he took was a strategy.

Everything he did had the potential to turn into something sinister.

When I'd go to bed at night, he was always the one to settle me to sleep. He would climb into bed beside me and offer to read a story but with one hand burrowing its way underneath the duvet, while the other held the book upright.

He'd stay for a half an hour or so, until any chance of me falling asleep had been destroyed, and then he would gratify himself. I was his to abuse.

I was about ten years old when we moved. By this time, I was mentally unwell. Many mornings through my childhood and teenage years, I used to wake up and I could not recognise my own speaking voice. It never sounded like me. It was a different person; a nicer person. When this voice would appear, I would talk or sing just to hear it. I had no idea why it happened, but it was strange, a bit scary, but also a novelty.

It was like I had another person inside me, but I was in control of this other person. This voice was more like another version of me. A nice me. One I liked. I controlled her and made the words that I wanted to hear, but she had a nicer voice, a kinder voice, a sweeter voice. But it wasn't my voice. My voice was horrible. I was a crow, and common when I spoke. This was a completely different one, not even like me when I spoke—it was a posh voice. It only ever came out when I was alone in my bedroom, either talking to myself, playing a game or singing. Then I would hear the nice voice come out and I would keep talking or singing, just to hear it. I liked this new voice and it stayed with me until I was about 13. I didn't notice when it went away. It just never came back.

I think it's likely that this was the voice of my 'inner child', the person I might have been if my father hadn't stolen my childhood. This was literally the child inside me trying to come out. It was the child I repressed because an abused child is one who has lost their innocence. My spirit kept fighting to break out, until I finally learned to silence her. She was not to awaken for many years to come.

*

My self-esteem continued to plummet after we moved house. I felt that I didn't fit in with the other kids in Castleknock. They all talked with posh accents. Da re-inforced this notion that I was an inferior girl because I spoke with a Dublin accent. He really never stopped telling me that people and strangers wouldn't respect me and that I wouldn't get a job if people thought I was common.

I had long stopped caring about my education by this time and didn't really think anything of the school I had been sent to.

I made a couple of friends when I entered the school but I didn't let anyone get close to me. The girls were nice kids but they lived in a different world to me. Although I was someone who picked up accents easily, I tried my hardest not to pick up theirs. It wasn't that I didn't think they had nice ones, I just wanted to rebel against everything.

I had come to hate and detest everything my father approved of. As far as he was concerned, people were not good enough unless they pronounced their words properly and measured up to an invisible yardstick he used.

In time, this sense of rebelliousness intensified. I'm still not sure whether this was a cry for help, or that I simply did not want to conform, but I refused to do anything that was asked of me.

I was ten years old and in sixth class but I discovered that *I* was the only thing that I could control.

My education was the first thing to suffer as a consequence of my new found liberty. I fell behind in my schoolwork for the first time because my mind was filled with such bad feelings that I no longer cared.

I also grew to hate Castleknock because Da loved it. From my point of view, his fuck-off house represented everything that was bad in this world. I hated it and him. I hated the fucking ground that he walked on.

But it was at this stage that my life also began to fall apart. You might say that I became dysfunctional though I would counter that I became functional in order to survive.

No one realised what was happening to me, so no one offered to help. My teachers found themselves having to deal with an unruly student who looked for trouble.

I also distanced myself from other girls at the school. I was terrified that if I got close to them, Da would too, and then I'd lose them all eventually.

I was always on guard, waiting for someone to blow my cover by pointing a finger at me and yelling, 'Look! There it is—the dirt! See how dirty she is.'

This became an obsession of mine. I used to wonder if anyone knew what he did to me. The truth was that nobody knew. I remember seeing Da laughing with some people one day and my mind had become so distorted that I was convinced he was telling them exactly what I let him do to me. Of course he wasn't, and they hadn't a clue what was going on, but I thought they were laughing at me, the dirty little bitch. My stomach churned and I felt hot and humiliated.

At other times, I would wonder when Da would be arrested for being a pervert. I remember one day the gardaí came to the school about some suspicious man who'd been seen in the area. All I could think was, 'Here we go again! Me fucking Da is at it again.'

I didn't want to hear the details of the car or anything that might confirm it was him. It wasn't Da but I assumed it was. My abiding memory of that event is of not being afraid of meeting the strange man the other girls feared. I wasn't afraid because I believed I knew him already.

I gave up on life in my last year of primary school. I stopped going to school by pretending to be sick. When I did attend class, I never paid any attention to my teacher or did my homework so it made no difference whether I was there or not.

Ma would ask me about homework, but I would either answer that I had none or that I'd done it already.

The abuse altered my life in every conceivable way. I never slept at night. If Da abused me, I would inevitably stay awake all night thinking about what he'd done. If he didn't happen to enter my room on a particular night, I would stay awake for fear that he was about to arrive. I lived in a state of perpetual fear.

The lack of sleep had an adverse effect on my intellectual development.

It also caused me to develop serious psychological problems.

The effect of sleep deprivation was obvious. I would waken each morning barely able to concentrate or focus on anything. Instead I would struggle to wake up, make my way downstairs and spoon Rice Krispies into my mouth while Da sat across from me, acting normal, like the previous night's events had never happened.

In fact, he sometimes shouted at me for causing him to run late.

It was around this time that I began to develop serious behavioural and psychological problems. Given that I had no control over my body, I began to control everything else by organising strict rituals which allowed me to exercise some control over my life.

At breakfast time, I would only eat from a certain bowl and use a certain spoon to eat. If breakfast was given to me in another bowl, I would refuse to eat it.

Of course, the bowl which I chose to eat from was old and battered. The spoon was equally battered—it was covered in sharp edges from where the garbage-disposal unit in the kitchen sink had swallowed the spoon so often that it was barely safe to use now. But I didn't care. To me, the bowl and spoon were like a rattler to a baby—soothing and comforting.

I ate my breakfast from that bowl and spoon every single morning, right up until I was married and had my first child.

I would then move on to my next ritual. Each morning, I would flatten the Rice Krispies in just the right way as they floated in a bowl. I would never swallow a spoonful until I had it perfect. Even the milk had to be just the right temperature and volume or I wouldn't go to school. And after every spoonful of cereal, I had to rotate the bowl a few degrees. I ate my breakfast in this exact way for more than 30 years.

My life quickly began to revolve around daily rituals. It was unnatural but it was a ten-year-old girl's way of remaining sane.

Behavioural and psychological problems were not the only issues I faced. My body started to turn against me, and I stopped being able to hold down food.

After breakfast each morning, I would go to the toilet and puke up my breakfast. I never made myself sick. My stomach just turned every morning after breakfast had been served and everything would come flying back up again.

I inevitably started to lose weight which affected my periods. It was awful.

I was quite young when I got my first period—I was only about ten years of age. In the beginning, my periods were so heavy that they lasted two weeks out of every four.

I was only 12 years old when I had a womb scraping done in an effort to get to the root of the pains that troubled me.

After school, if I even went that is, I'd collapse with exhaustion on the sofa and sleep for the rest of the evening. I was so tired from the lack of sleep, lack of food, and stress.

At one stage, I was diagnosed as suffering from anorexia although I did eat. My stomach just turned as soon as it saw food. I didn't want to be sick. I didn't like the feeling—it just happened.

I had long since learned how to separate body and mind so I no longer had a rational thought process—I just did things as my subconscious dictated.

Fake pains and real pains—I stopped being able to tell them apart.

I was taken to hospital on countless occasions and underwent surgery for mysterious illnesses.

I induced cramps and severe pains in the hope that a doctor would be able to get rid of the physical pain in my guts, then maybe, while they were in there, they'd also be able to take away the dark, empty blackness that sometimes accompanied this pain.

Or at least give me some tablets that would make it all better. And that would be the end of these bad feelings—the pain I couldn't explain.

On one occasion a surgeon operated on me because I had complained so much about the pain, but nothing of medical significance was found. I still complained of a pain afterwards though.

I can honestly say though that even if the doctors and nurses had asked me the right questions, I wouldn't have told them anything. If a social worker had called to my house, I would have done everything I could to hide the truth. If they'd asked me if my father was sexually abusing me, I would have smiled sweetly and said, 'No, nothing is happening.'

Da knew this. It would have killed me to have been taken from my home. I'd have lost more than I would have chosen to lose. What little control I had would also have been removed.

I never linked all the illnesses—both real and perceived—to the abuse until I was an adult.

The depression, the fake pains, vomiting and the inexplicable pains were all completely separate as far as I was concerned. I was one hurt little girl yet I still helped prevent Da's dirty little secret from getting out. I thought I was doing a great job 'cause no one ever asked any questions.

The rest of the family looked upon Da as an honest and good man because they didn't know the truth. No one knew what he was doing. Our family was a success. I didn't want to be the one to put my hand up in the air and cause our family express train to come screeching to a halt.

*

It was during a family holiday to France that I began to understand exactly what lengths my father would go to in order to gratify himself. That summer, he brought a trailer tent and took us on holiday to France.

The trip was memorable for two reasons. The first was the ferry crossing which caused me to get seasick. The second reason why I remember that holiday is that it was the first time that Da found it difficult to conceal his sexual interest in me.

all my fault

My family spent the holiday travelling from campsite to campsite. We made friends with lots of other families, of all different nationalities. I met other girls of all ages, who Da also befriended.

I don't know if he abused any of them but I suspect that he did.

I can recall watching him scan the campsite for little girls whom he could encourage me to talk to.

He would get as close to these children as he could. He might suggest that we go to the swimming pool or play together.

He would put blankets over them, offering to help make them 'cosy' when they emerged from the water.

Prior to this holiday, Da had always used me for his own sexual gratification. He considered my body to be a tool which he used to pleasure himself. He never really looked at me or my body but all that changed during our holiday to France.

Throughout the holiday, Da found it difficult to conceal his sexual interest in me. In fact, he hardly took his eyes off me. Everywhere I went his eyes followed, looking me up and down before coming to rest around my chest area.

I found this terrifying and revolting. And with reason; what if he went further than he had before and got me pregnant? He also began talking to me in a way that made my skin crawl. He constantly made remarks about how I was changing physically.

'Oh, look how your little buds are growing,' he said whilst leering at me.

One day he went further and touched my breasts in public as if I was enjoying his attention.

To stop him, I decided to wear as many clothes as possible that covered my body. I started wearing a 70s-style long red cardigan, and refused to take it off. This became a huge bone of contention between me and my mother.

She couldn't understand why I refused to wear the new clothes that she bought me to wear on the holiday—halternecks, shorts and skirts.

As far as I was concerned, wearing these clothes was tantamount to inviting trouble. The red cardigan covered up everything. While I couldn't stop him from molesting me, I could stop him looking at me.

I thought that if I could make my body invisible then maybe Da might leave me alone for a while and let me enjoy my holiday. But I should have known that would never happen.

That holiday also stands out because it was the first time that Da took risks to abuse me.

At the time, I thought I would be relatively safe because we were all crowded into a two-room trailer tent. Ma and Da slept on one side and we slept on a double mattress on the other side. But one night, Da got undressed and came over to our side of the tent and climbed into bed beside me. He was talking away, asking me and my brothers what we thought of the holiday so far and if we were having fun, when all of a sudden I felt his hand tugging at my knickers underneath the blankets. He started rubbing my vagina and prised my legs apart so he could push his fingers inside me. All the while he chatted away to my brothers as if nothing was happening.

I was so shocked that I didn't know what to think. I just lay there, trying to concentrate on what my brothers were saying. Five minutes previously I had been like any other child, happily discussing the day with my brothers. Now I just lay there like a zombie trying to project my mind to a different place.

This happened a few times on the holiday, with my brothers lying inches away. They were oblivious to what was happening. It was humiliating for me. I felt so used, like an inanimate object that my da made use of when it suited him.

But it also made me angry. I hated it and when he molested me in such circumstances, it proved to me that I was being used. This was a turning point.

We did lots of touristy things on that holiday. We visited the Louvre Gallery; we ate croissants for breakfast and tasted frogs' legs and snails but I can't remember how any of these smelled, tasted or felt. What I do remember, and will never forget, is how it felt to have Da climb under the covers beside me at night, rubbing his body parts all over me and soiling all the good memories of the day in the process.

There were other family holidays that I did enjoy, however, simply because Da wasn't there. We went to Butlins on holidays for a week every year, but Da usually stayed at home for most of this week. I loved going to Butlins, not only for the obvious reasons, such as having fun with my friends, but because it was a break from being abused. I could be a real little girl in Butlins, concerned only with sweets, the fair ground and playing the day away.

We had pretty much a free reign there. At home I was always so tired and sleepy during the day; at Butlins the energy flowed through me.

all my fault

I always made new friends, and was teased mercilessly because if I hung around with people from Cork I came home with a Cork accent, if they were Northerners I came home with a twang as if I had lived in Belfast all my life. But what got to Da was when I would hang around with a crowd from Dublin's inner city. He knew I was playing with them when I came back because my accent would go downhill, in his opinion.

I had a Dublin accent anyway but he hated it. At one point he became so ashamed of me that he sent me to elocution lessons. He didn't realise that the accents were not something I did deliberately. It was something I got teased with for years but I was not pretending. My voice just took over and copied what it heard. I pretty much speak the same now as I did when I was four, so I'm not sure the elocution lessons made much of an impact on me.

I was particularly deflated at the end of those holidays. For me it was not just that the fun was over, it also meant back to reality; back to the nightmare of being sexually abused by Da.

Chapter Five

Not unexpectedly, I was asked to repeat sixth class because I had missed so many days at school. The request, which was justifiable, caught me by surprise and reinforced the belief that existed in my own mind that there was something wrong with me; that I was dirty and deserving of what Da did to me. I was a failure in school, and it was official as far as the other girls were concerned. This reinforced my negative feelings about myself.

I did as I was asked and repeated the year but it proved to be a futile exercise. I didn't learn much and I was miserable and lonely. Even when other girls in the class tried to reach out to me, I pulled even further away. I was old enough now to know that I had to keep these girls away from my house at any cost.

This was hard when they were always calling for me and I would have given anything to have friends. When they stopped calling to play, I became even more withdrawn from everyone and everything.

The pain inside me just never seemed to go away. While I thought that I shouldn't have been feeling so lonely and insecure, I did not understand why I felt the way I did. I knew the world was meant to be a happy place and fathers were supposed to be faithful and loyal to their children. But my world was different; I lived in a dark dysfunctional world where life wasn't that simple.

Inside I felt dead; I existed in an upside-down world where I was humiliated on a nightly basis by the man who was supposed to protect me. Yet I suffered to protect him because he was my father.

I was a 12-year-old girl who got what she deserved because there was no other explanation to explain my predicament.

By this time, I had become more physically and mentally ill. Even if I'd looked for help, I felt that no one would have believed me.

I was a confused child, who believe it or not, thought I deserved what Da did to me and I was the bad one.

When I think of that little girl, I wish I could sit and talk to her and comfort her. I wish I could make her see that her father was not worth having; that he was an animal and an abuser.

Such wishes are nothing more than fanciful notions to me now. At the time though, I convinced myself that there was something horrible about me that made him do this to me; if I am to be honest I believed he wasn't at fault.

In time, my life became so bad that I couldn't cope anymore. I decided that I had to stop the pain somehow and permanently. The doctors had tried everything to cure me medically and nothing had worked so I saw only one other option—that was to take my own life. This was not the momentous decision that you might think. Children don't understand the finality of death. I certainly didn't. I believed suicide was something that people made a fuss about, but I didn't understand why. It wasn't something that I thought through or even wanted. It was, I suppose, a cry for help albeit a serious one.

If I remember what happened correctly, I decided to take my own life on the spur of the moment while I was feeling low one day.

The memory of this event has faded with time but I can remember searching my house for tablets and medicines when everyone was out, gathering up every single tablet I could find. I am sure that I was in the depths of depression though I didn't know what depression was. I did, however, know that I didn't want to feel so low anymore. Swallowing enough tablets to kill myself was one way to escape; that was my reckoning.

Thankfully the tablets I gathered weren't enough to kill me. When I had gathered up what I considered to be enough pills, I swallowed them all one by one and sat down and waited for the pain to end. In my mind I had this beautiful feeling that would be just like the escape the anaesthetic gave me before I had an operation, the peace to fall asleep without struggling and a release from thinking and feeling bad thoughts and a period of absolutely no pain.

It didn't happen like this though. I lay on the ground at home crippled with pains in my stomach and disorientated. Ma came in and asked what was wrong with me. I just told her that I had severe pains. I think she could see that it was more serious than a simple stomach ache, as she immediately took me to the doctor.

I didn't tell anyone what I had done though, least of all Ma, because I knew that would be the start of questions I couldn't answer. Or questions that I would have preferred not to answer. My recollections of this time are still hazy but I do recall clearly what happened to me a few days later.

Life returned to normal—or what counted for normal in my life—very fast.

Da didn't leave me alone even though he knew I had just been unwell. It didn't matter whether I was sick or even if I was a young girl suffering from a heavy period, he still came into my room and climbed into bed beside me as always. The abuse continued. The sick bastard needed his gratification and I was there to provide it.

*

My journey towards self-destruction continued unabated. With the passing of time, I became even more disturbed and mentally ill.

I couldn't eat properly, suffered from phantom pains and illnesses, and developed more serious behavioural disorders.

On top of that, some of the other kids couldn't understand how I was sick so often, and how I seemed to be off school so much. My trips to the hospital and doctors naturally affected my relationships, as children have short memories and like to play with children if they are there. I was spending so much time 'sick' at home or in hospital that I was deemed 'different' to the other kids. Some of them would taunt me, disbelieving that I was really sick. They called me a liar and said that I was only pretending to be sick so I wouldn't have to go to school. I was so confused by this, because in my heart I knew that they were telling the truth; I wasn't sick in the way that I pretended to be. But I did need help. I did need someone to look after me, and these pains and illnesses in my head and in my heart transferred themselves into my body.

I hated being called a liar, more than anything, and most of all it made me realise that people might not believe me if I said anything about my da abusing me. If they thought I was lying about having pains in my stomach, what would they think if I said that my da came into my room at night? That he would take off my pyjama bottoms and knickers, and put his big, fat fingers into my vagina, roughly pushing them in, bruising me inside; that even when I pretended to be asleep, he would lift my floppy body, and rub his hard erection against me?

*

As I said earlier, one way in which the abuse affected me was to create a series of behavioural problems, over which I had no control. These behavioural problems were all-consuming and possessed me. They finished off what was left of my childhood and caused me to fall even lower into a mire of depression, self-doubt and anxiety.

I was consumed by phobias. One of these, more than any other, practically crippled me and ruined my life. It was a fear of hair strands. I developed a phobia of hair because my da's pubic hair would often be left behind on my bedsheets and it used to make me feel physically sick to see them. This phobia then transferred to hair of all type. I became fixated on making sure that I did not come into contact with loose hair strands be they on someone's shoulder, or on a chair or anywhere else.

As time passed, I got to the stage I forced myself to check my own clothes every night and morning to make sure that none of my own hair or anyone else's was loose around me.

I had a talent, if you could call it that, of knowing immediately if a strand of hair was loose or attached to someone's head. I could even tell with my own hair, when it was resting on my shoulders, if any strands were loose.

If I found a loose hair, I could not relax unless I had placed it in a bin. If I was sitting behind someone on a bus or in the cinema say, and there was a hair on that person's coat, I would feel sick and have to move as far away from them as I could.

The problem became so chronic and out of control, that at times I used to sit for hours just running my hands through my own hair, searching for a strand that felt unnatural or different to me. Although I was born with blonde hair, I gradually came to hate hair strands which I considered to be of a different colour, thickness or texture.

If I found a black or dark-coloured hair, I would pull it out. I now realise this was a form of self-mutilation in so far that I was hurting myself, but at the time it felt like the most natural thing in the world.

If you haven't suffered from an irrational fear, then it is hard to understand how awful this behaviour can become and how it affects people.

My whole day was controlled by this fear. Of course, once other children discovered this weakness or character flaw, it was used against me. They would leave hair strands on my belongings in the knowledge that it would upset me. Of course they didn't understand the seriousness of my phobia or what it stemmed from; they simply thought it was funny.

I never associated my phobias or rituals with the abuse. But later, while in counselling, I found out that my subconscious was using these irrational fears to deal with the more rational ones I was being forced to confront.

Self-harm, be it mental or physical, is actually simple to understand.

By pulling out my own hair and creating phobias, my subconscious was channelling my father's depravations into a form that I could deal with and even control to a certain extent.

My fixation with hair allowed me to regain some control, or, to a 12-year-old girl, to run in the other direction if I came into contact with loose strands of hair. Unfortunately, or tragically for me, I was too young to run away from my father.

*

That summer we went to Spain on holidays. This time my parents decided we would fly, as everyone had been so sick on the boat when we travelled to France. I was so excited to be going on a plane, as it was my first time.

Unfortunately the pleasure of flying was disrupted by an unmerciful sharp pain in my ears that brought me to tears. But even though the nice lady gave us sweets to suck for the landing and take off, I couldn't stand the pain and was glad to get off the plane when it landed.

We arrived by bus to some holiday resort. I made friends and played by the pool. This is one holiday that I really don't have any more good memories about, despite staying there for two full weeks. In fact, I don't have any memories of it, except for one, and this one I would happily delete from my mind if I could.

Somehow I got really badly sunburnt, even though Ma had covered me in lotion before going outside. When we got back to the apartment, Ma covered me in more lotion that night to help with the sunburn, but it still hurt to move.

My shoulders were blistered, and I wouldn't stop complaining about how badly it hurt. I wanted Da to know how much pain I was in, so that he might leave me alone. I should have known that it wouldn't make any difference to him.

That night, Ma and Da went to their double bedroom, the boys had their own separate bedroom and I slept in the sitting room on a convertible couch. I remember waiting and hoping that he wouldn't come near me. But he did. I didn't have the wallpaper to tear or anything familiar to do. So I just played asleep like I had done millions of times before. He undressed me and dropped my pants to the floor. He was already naked. He pulled me on top of him, even though I was completely limp. He did all the actions, pulling me up and down on him. I was lying on top, floppy and not moving, pretending to be asleep as usual, being pulled up and down, up and down along his body. I could feel his erect penis and it disgusted me.

I remember the stinging sensation as he did what he wanted to do and that, in a way, was a welcome distraction. It took my mind off him. He left and as I lay on my back, with my skin so sensitive, the tears silently fell down the side of my face. I couldn't move I was so sore. I remember both ears had a pool of tears collected in them. That's my biggest memory of Spain.

*

The passing of each year brought more misery to my life. I came bottom of the class after repeating sixth class. Spending another year in primary school had been a waste of time. The only discipline that interested me was essay writing. It was the one thing that I enjoyed in school as it allowed me to escape into a world of creativity. Apart from this, my life continued to deteriorate, primarily because my father's abuse became more intense and invasive. His sexual interest in me intensified because I had started to become a young woman. Contrary to what you might have expected, the start of puberty didn't turn my father off.

I believe it encouraged him even more. In fact, there were times when his predations became so bad that I felt like murdering him. I wished that something awful would happen to him, that he would die and I'd be rid of him forever.

I had never experienced utter hatred for anyone or anything prior to this but I developed pure hatred for that bastard when I entered my teens.

I think the onset of adulthood triggered off in me a sense of confidence that had so far been missing. I did not understand anything of such emotions at the time but within the space of a year I had found the courage to confront him.

Chapter Six

Despite my poor performance in primary school, I started secondary school when I was 12, attending Mount Sackville, a private school which lies adjacent to the Phoenix Park.

Da told his friends that he chose the school to give me a good start in life. I guessed that he wanted to make a lady out of me; that I'd graduate with perfect grammar and a nice accent.

Whether or not I received a good education was irrelevant. My memory of that time is one of not really caring what happened. I certainly never thought about my options.

In my mind, I already knew what I wanted to be when I grew up—I wanted to be a writer.

I wanted to marry a farmer and live on his farm, surrounded by animals, while I would write during the day. Though at some point, I did also want to become a vet.

In the end, my education became an irrelevancy. I spent

weeks at home suffering from phantom pains and illnesses during my first year in secondary school. It was the usual story.

I complained of aches and pains until a doctor finally admitted me to hospital for tests. I was subjected to every conceivable type of medical test until they could do no more. Finally they said they couldn't find anything wrong with me.

My poor mother would have to traipse up and down to the hospital several times a day, bringing me Lucazode and food from home.

You might ask if I consciously lied insofar that I claimed to feel pain when there was none. This wasn't the case. The pains I experienced were very real to me. I don't know whether I imagined them or convinced myself of their existence but I certainly felt them.

My infrequent appearances at school made sure that I never made many friends, though I did become close to one girl. Her name was *Dara* and the two of us became great friends.

We spent most of the time talking about the boys we liked, clothes, music and makeup. She knew nothing of my private circumstances but her friendship became one of the few things in life that mattered to me.

I just went through the motions of attending school Monday to Friday. I never did any homework and I rarely ever opened my school books, so when it came to questions in class I just tried to keep my head low and avoided making eye contact with the teacher.

I also got into trouble with teachers. One incident

happened during sports day when my brother and some of his friends came to visit.

I had my hair coloured pink for the big day. A nun eventually caught me and expelled me. I was told to go home but I didn't care.

As far as I was concerned, managing to get expelled from school gave me a new-found sense of credibility. I wasn't embarrassed by it at the time, although I am now when I think back on how I behaved.

I never liked Mount Sackville, not that there was anything wrong with the school. I just didn't like it because Da had decided to send me there. To me, the school represented his plans for my future. As far as I was concerned, anything that he endorsed was to be rejected. This became my philosophy on life.

*

By the time I turned 13, I had become so damaged that Da knew the suffering his abuse caused me; but he was a paedophile and I was his victim. If he did think of the damage he was doing to me, he either didn't care or was so sexually aroused by me that he couldn't stop himself.

So my life fell apart and any future I had went with it. I spent most days watching TV and drifting in and out of sleep, making excuses that I couldn't go to school because I was sick, or because my period pains were so bad.

This became another routine. I would watch television all day, then, in the evening time, Da's key would turn in the door and I'd jolt awake.

I would say nothing to him. He would just look at me. He would then eat his dinner and go up to bed for a short lie-down. Later on, he'd come back downstairs wearing just a wine and navy dressing gown, sometimes wearing nothing underneath.

He'd pour himself either a brandy or a Southern Comfort and he'd sit on the couch, his legs spread wide and the dressing gown gaping open as he talked to me. I'd try not to look at him for fear of arousing him.

His favourite topic of conversation was, more often than not, how great he was. How he was a better father than any of the other dads I knew.

How he wasn't down in the pub getting drunk at the weekends like the rest of them. He liked to tell me that he was one of the cleverest, most intelligent men I would ever meet.

Eventually, I'd go to bed, knowing he wouldn't be long. He'd usually come up on to the landing when we were all tucked in, me in my room and the boys in theirs, and he'd read a book from the *Just William* collection or some funny poetry like those by Pam Ayres.

When he was finished, I'd lie in wait. He'd come in, close the door gently behind him and get into bed beside me, on the pretext of snuggling me. The sexual assault would then begin.

When he was done, when the bastard had satisfied himself, he'd leave as if all he had done to me was just give me a normal goodnight kiss.

*

I felt my sanity slipping further and further away. I had become a suicidal 13-year-old and I knew that if my father continued to abuse me I would breakdown. When a child is forced to confront danger, they tend to run to their parents for comfort and protection. I was not in a position to do this. I felt that if I had told anyone what my father was doing, I would have broken my family. So I turned to myself for help and discovered in me the strength to say no, to fight him off and confront the monster who was my father.

One night, moments after Da came into my bedroom, I decided to say no. I can remember that night as vividly as if it happened yesterday.

The door opened slightly and he stepped into the room and began to move towards my bed. He was naked underneath that horrible familiar dressing gown which was open.

As he closed the door, I sat up and pulled the duvet tightly around me.

He took a few steps towards me, bent down and attempted to pull the blankets back.

'No!'

The word just came out of my mouth. He was stunned. Even in the darkness I could see that he was taken aback and did not know what to say or do.

He stood there naked. Then he just turned and left. That was it. It was over.

I was overcome by a mixture of emotions. The first was one of relief. Then fear. Then I was overwhelmed by a complete disgust and anger at myself for not having said

'No' sooner. Da had never threatened me with violence or coerced me into letting him abuse me.

I could have said 'No' before but I hadn't. Instead I had chosen to let guilt and shame rest on my shoulders. I did, however, take solace from the fact that Da could no longer abuse me and would be too afraid to enter my room again. I soon learned that he had other ideas. If he couldn't touch, he decided that he could look.

*

I hadn't tried to stop my father or fend him off before this night because he was a man who I was conditioned to love. Everyone in the family loved Da. Ma loved him. My brothers loved him. He was a success story.

I was taught to respect, love and fear him in equal measures. I was never told not to trust him or to question his motives. He was after all my father.

Nor had I the confidence and experience to see him for what he was, or even to understand what he was doing to me.

I didn't know what a paedophile was; I had never even heard the word.

No one had told me that some men, be they fathers, teachers or priests, were sexually attracted to young children. I was a child after all, and knew nothing of such matters.

All I knew was that my father made me feel dirty, repulsive and inhuman when he molested me but I believed that was my problem and not his.

So I continued to suffer from depression and low self-esteem even though he had stopped abusing me.

In fact, I would go as far as to say that the sense of relief that I experienced when I said no was just temporary.

You might say that I felt like a dog which had been kept on a tight leash, only to have the owner replace it with a 50-foot chain.

As far as I was concerned, I hadn't been freed, and the problem hadn't been solved, but my situation wasn't as bad as it had been.

I could at least pretend to be free but whenever I walked past the 50-foot mark, the chain would yank me back to reality. To me, the threat posed by my father remained very real. The threat that he represented was always there, lurking in the shadows. In time, I would come to learn that the threat of a sexual attack was just as debilitating as the abuse itself.

In this regard, I remained a deeply disturbed child. I still suffered from phobias and lived a life which revolved around the rituals that my subconscious used to keep me sane.

I continued to search my immediate environment for loose strands of hair; I continued to pull my own hair out; I ate my breakfast in the exact same way each morning only to eject the contents of my stomach minutes later.

Because I made sure that I never went to school, I spent my afternoons sleeping.

Even though Da had stopped coming into my room at night, I still could not sleep. I feared that I would wake up in the room with him there. During this time, when I look back on those years between the ages of three and thirteen, I don't see the memories clearly like I do with memories of other years. It's like I remember everything from inside my head, looking out. I wasn't there in person or in spirit, but I could see everything. I was hiding in my own head.

In physical terms, it would be like looking through a pair of binoculars: you have a distant, tunnel vision. That's how I remember those years. I was literally inside looking out, through the holes in my eyes.

*

I wasn't naturally a rebellious teenager but I became one by the time I reached 14 years. I don't know whether I would have acted differently if my childhood had been a normal one though.

I am certain that I would have studied harder if my father hadn't abused me.

As for the life I led for the remainder of my teenage years I can only guess, though I suspect the abuse did encourage me to start drinking and rebelling against authority while I was still at school.

The rebellion began in earnest when I started to drink. I never had difficulty buying beer when I was young. In fact, it was relatively easy to get someone to buy alcohol in an off-licence. All I had to do was to ask people walking in the door to buy me a flagon of cider and they generally obliged.

I never drank at home. Instead, I opted to drink in the fields and woodlands around west Dublin with a gang of locals that I'd become friends with. We'd sit around talking, laughing, drinking, getting off with boys and basically getting pissed out of our heads. It was best described as teenage hedonism. I didn't care what anyone thought of me. All I cared about was doing what I wanted.

I was to some extent a teenage delinquent and was out of control. I didn't care about school, had suicidal tendencies and hated authority of any kind.

To this day, I still don't know how I wasn't caught drinking. There were nights when gardaí were called to move us from parklands where we were drinking and I was very nearly arrested.

Whenever the police would arrive, someone would scream 'RAID'. We'd all run in different directions through the woods around the River Tolka, one place that we used to frequent, hoping that we wouldn't be caught.

I'd just find a good hiding spot and lie low till the danger had passed.

Ironically, drinking cider in fields and woods gave some purpose to my life. I started to look forward to the weekends and it helped numb that pain in my heart that threatened to overwhelm me.

Getting completely pissed out of my head became an anaesthetic of sorts. It enabled me to cope with the bullshit that I had to deal with. I also started to smoke around this time. This wasn't just normal teenage rebellion—I knew how much Da despised people who smoked, so it made each puff more enjoyable.

*

In many ways my life was in a state of freefall. But the worst aspect to my life continued to be Da, whom I had to face every day. I found living under the same roof as him to be an ordeal in itself.

I had come to despise and hate him. Living in close proximity to him made me feel insecure and uneasy. He made my skin crawl.

The worst thing was the pretence that each of us adopted. I acted as if everything was okay and he acted as if he was a loving father. He smiled at me and I smiled back. We both acted out the roles of father and daughter as if our relationship was a normal one.

We were all one big happy family. Only Da and I knew the truth. And if we kept silent, then everything else would be okay. There were even times when I tried to convince myself that I could erase the past for the sake of my family.

Then I saw him looking at me through the glass window over my door. My bedroom had a small glass panel above the door to allow light into the hallway, but you wouldn't be able to see in to my room without standing on something.

I cannot explain why my attention was drawn to the window, but as I was getting undressed in my room one night, I felt that someone was watching me.

I looked up and saw Da standing on his large stepladder. I scrambled for my clothes the second I saw him and dived under the bed covers. He didn't seem bothered that I'd discovered him and it was only when he was sure that the show was definitely over that he climbed down. As soon as he was gone, I tore down posters of Phil Lynott and Leif

Garrett from the wall and used them to cover the window. I made sure that there wasn't even the tiniest gap between them.

The next day, Da came storming in and ripped them all down with the excuse that the landing was too dark and needed the light coming from my bedroom. I went to Ma in floods of tears and pretended that the light bulb on the landing was shining into my room at night and keeping me awake. She sided with me and the posters went back up.

The installation of peep-holes was Da's response. He made the peep-holes after he disappeared up into the attic one night. Our attic was just a normal one though it was much larger than that of your average house. It was filled with old Christmas decorations, camping gear and other half-forgotten rubbish that we didn't want to throw away.

It didn't even have a proper floor—it just had beams that you had to try and balance on, otherwise your foot might go through the ceiling of a bedroom.

I can only assume that Da had watched me undress on numerous occasions before I noticed him as he only began venturing into the attic after I blocked out the bedroom window.

Like everything my father did, it appeared innocuous at first.

Every evening, he would get up on his old painting ladder, which had now become a permanent fixture on the landing, and climb up into the attic. I thought nothing of it when I heard the sound of him drilling; that was until I saw tiny holes in the bathroom ceiling which he used to watch me going to the toilet or taking a shower.

Having my privacy robbed was a whole new type of violation that I couldn't comprehend.

Even after all these years, it is hard to describe how humiliated I felt each time I had to undress. I would stare at these tiny holes wondering if he was looking at me. Not knowing was just as bad as knowing that he was there. If I went to the toilet, I would stare at a hole trying to see if he was there, watching in silence.

It was at this point I decided to try to stop him. I refused to let him look at me. I undressed under the dressing table from then on, knowing that he was in the attic. I started bringing an umbrella into the toilet, especially when I had my period. I never accepted that he could just watch me, I just didn't always know where the holes were.

This new invasion of privacy started messing with my head. Eventually I became certain that he could see everything I did, from scratching my head to undressing. I even felt like he could read my thoughts so I tried to keep my mind as blank as possible. I felt transparent. It was like Da owned every single part of me—mind, body and soul—and there was nothing left for me.

Then I would ask myself if I was being paranoid. When I felt really low I'd even ask if it was wrong for him to watch me? He wasn't hurting me physically; he wasn't touching me; so why did I feel so degraded and humiliated?

The only respite I got at this stage was at the weekends when he and Ma would spend their free time on their boat on the Shannon. This was Da's latest show of materialistic bullshit. He couldn't wait to show off his new purchase, and he used to show photographs of it to all his friends. He embraced this lifestyle by wearing a captain's hat, as well as buying a whole new wardrobe full of clothes, complete with boaty shoes. I grew to hate navy, white and red as they reminded me of him. He even developed a new 'boaty' language where everything was nautical.

I had to go down to Shannon the first few weekends, but I hated it. Everyone slept in the one room, and Da wouldn't give me any privacy to get changed, so I just stayed in my pyjamas all day. He was embarrassed by this as he spent a lot of time socialising down there, and he didn't want people to see his teenage daughter hanging around in her pj's. So he agreed that I didn't have to go with them on their weekend jaunts.

I spent those weekends having parties and generally going wild drinking and smoking hash, unbeknownst to my parents. Every Sunday evening I would clean the house in a panic, going so far as to burn toast, so that it would hide the smell of cigarette smoke.

The familiar knot of tension would reappear on a Sunday evening as Da walked back through the door. I always made sure I was already changed into my pyjamas when he came in, so his trip to the attic that night would be a wasted one.

Chapter Seven

Da's career continued to go from strength to strength. Around this time, he was made president of some professional body.

This was the icing on the cake for him; this was the moment he had waited for all his life. Jesus, like I hadn't heard enough about how amazing and hard working he was and how the two sets of relations from either side of the family weren't a patch on him.

Da may have been a paedophile, but he was also a snob. He criticised everything and everyone. He reminded me of one of the gossipy characters from a soap opera, someone who judged everyone.

He was in many ways a strange man. He had a particular grudge against people who smoked for example. They were ignorant and brainless according to him, even though his own mother smoked. She even tried to keep it a secret from him. Having reared him and having worked hard all her life, she was too afraid to let him down by smoking a cigarette.

When she stayed over in our house, she'd have a puff or two and smoke out the window of my bedroom, like a teenager trying to hide her habit from her parents.

I remember one time when she was smoking in my room, she must have thought she was about to be caught because she sprayed a thick mist of deodorant all around the room to hide the smell of smoke.

I had two goldfish in a bowl on my dressing table at the time and I found them the next morning lying belly-up. There was a thick oily film on top of the bowl and when I dipped my finger in it I found it had a floral smell. I think the deodorant killed the poor things. But I felt more sorry for Nanny than the fish. I thought it was sad that she was afraid to embarrass her own son.

Everything revolved around status and money with my father. This attitude, which I despised, extended to everything and everyone.

Prospective boyfriends were scrutinised, not to see if they really liked me but to see if they were suitable to go out with me. He would ask where they lived, what their parents did, if they lived in a private or corporation house, and if it was a corporation house, had their parents bought it. The questions all revolved around what they had and where they came from. He didn't ask if they treated me well or if I liked them.

A person's class was more important to him than anything else. This really upset me, as it would have any teenager.

In fact, I used to find myself making up stories that people lived in private houses just to keep Da happy. I didn't give a shit about people's backgrounds, I just didn't want Da to be condescending towards them.

*

After I was expelled from Mount Sackville, I spent second and third year attending a school on North Great George's Street in central Dublin. I went on the hop and mitched so much there that the teachers hardly even knew my name.

I was now living a dysfunctional life and was out of control. If I didn't like the look of the weather when I got up in the morning, I'd say I was sick and stay at home for the day.

My time in this school passed without incident. In one way it took the heat off me, but at the same time, that was the kernel of the problem. I had the ability to learn and obtain good grades in school; it was just that everyone seemed to give up on me.

To say I was a loner in school is an understatement. I shunned friends and discouraged anyone who wanted to become close to me.

I was a disturbed teenager. I used to make up stories about myself and I found myself conjuring up a whole fantasy family life whenever I discussed my family. I'd lie about how many brothers I had, what my parents worked at and what a wonderful life I had led. I basically gave myself a whole new life that bore no similarity to my real one.

I don't know why I acted like this but it didn't take long for people to find out the truth and stop talking to me. So, as you might imagine, I didn't really socialise with the other girls.

Drawing attention to myself became an important focus in my life. I did everything and anything to get noticed.

One night, when I was feeling especially low, I took a pair of scissors to my hair and butchered it.

It was all patchy and in different lengths. I didn't feel very attractive on the inside so I didn't care what I looked like on the outside.

I can now see that I was trying to punish myself.

Da went mental when he saw me but I didn't care. In fact I was delighted at having pissed him off.

I wanted to look really ugly so he wouldn't want to look at me anymore. Of course, it made no difference. Da had his peep-holes at strategic locations around the house. If he wanted to look at me, I could do little to stop him.

*

By this time, Da had discovered that I was drinking, so he began to watch me closely and try to control me. I often wonder did Da know why I was going off the rails, or did he even care.

I personally believe he knew the abuse he inflicted on me had transformed me into a dysfunctional teenager but he didn't care. Da was driven by self-gratification; that is what drove him to abuse children.

Whether or not his daughter was suicidal was almost an irrelevancy. My memory of this time is one of utter loneliness.

Though I had friends outside of school, they were mainly drinking buddies. Sometimes, when I just wanted to escape, I'd tell my parents I was sleeping over in a friend's house. On those occasions, I'd go and buy some drink and spend the night sleeping rough, with only the alcohol to cushion me from the cold, hard ground. As far as I was concerned, it was better than being in a bed at home though and feeling Da's eyes staring down at me from the ceiling.

If I didn't have money for alcohol and I couldn't find any to steal from home, then I'd just go to my parents' drinks cabinet with an empty plastic bottle and fill it up.

Alcohol became my sedative. I didn't care what it tasted like. I would mix loads of different spirits together. More often than not, it would taste awful but it got me completely drunk, or out of my head.

I don't even remember getting hangovers. I never minded being out in the dark either. I was afraid of no one. I wasn't an aggressive person but if someone started a fight, small and all as I was, I could fight back and box their ears. But I never fought out of spite or anger. I just defended myself.

I remember the worst dig I ever got was from a girl from Blanchardstown in west Dublin. I had gone for a walk with some fella she fancied one Friday night, but all we'd done was sit in a field chatting while we drank a flagon of cider between us. But later on that night she marched over to me with her hands on her hips, her face scarlet with anger.

'You keep your hands off him unless I say you can have him. Right?' she said as she gave me the most unmerciful kick.

It took a few seconds for the pain to die down but when it did I jumped up and boxed the little bitch black and blue. I couldn't let her win. If she got the better of me once, there'd be no stopping her and she'd never leave me alone. From then on, nobody in that gang ever dared pick on me as that girl had been a toughie. If you could kick her ass in a fight then people knew not to mess with you. I developed a reputation for being tough, which was great because it meant people were too scared of me to ever try it on so I was rarely in any fights after that.

*

When I was 15, I started using acid when I began hanging around with a girl from Cabra. She was deadly craic. There was this lad she fancied from Phibsboro, on the north side of Dublin, so she introduced me to him and his mates. They were a few years older than us and were small-time drug dealers so I was a little intimidated by them when I first met them.

'How yis? Ye wanna hang out in town?' asked the taller one.

'I haven't got a bean. I've no odds at all,' I said.

'Sure don't worry. We have a few bob to collect and we won't leave ye stuck,' said the smaller one.

I knew he liked me straight away. I thought he was all right. He looked a little like Mick Jagger but he wasn't really my type. But I thought he was funny and I found it hard to resist people who could put a smile on my face.

Up to this point, I had drunk a lot of alcohol and

smoked a lot of hash, and when I couldn't manage to roll a joint, I would eat it. I'd go into the toilet, burn the hash with a lighter to soften it and crumple it into some tin foil before eating it. Smoking was better though, it gave you more of a buzz but I was crap at rolling a joint so sometimes it was easier just to eat it. People used to tease me that my catchphrase was, 'Here, I'll buy a spot off you if you roll them for me first.' I even bought a little machine to do the rolling but it was even more useless than me.

So we followed these guys up to a pool hall and watched as they collected money from different people and handed over small packages in return. We thought these guys were real bad asses so when we called up to one of their houses later we got the shock of our lives.

'Come on in girls and take a seat,' said a nice lady who turned out to be the mother of one of the guys.

'Will you have a cup of tea?'

'No thanks. I don't drink tea,' I replied.

'Are you one of those healthy-living people? You certainly look fit and what a lovely shine off your hair. Can I get you anything else love?'

She seemed like the nicest woman in the world. She clearly hadn't a clue what her son got up to when he was out of her sight.

'Bye bye love,' she said to her son as we were leaving, 'Have a nice time playing video games.'

We all headed into town to a games hall. It had video games in the front and snooker tables in the back. I used to be in there every second day back then when I was on the hop from school.

The lads pulled out what looked like sheets of cardboard with lots of tiny pictures of strawberries dotted all over them. They tore off two small squares and handed one to me and one to my mate. They told us to put them on our tongues and wait for the strawberry surprise. The surprise was the best fucking high I've ever had. My senses were heightened to the point where I thought I was going to become airborne. I felt like I could do absolutely anything.

The boys gave us each some money to play video games and I headed straight for Space Invaders. I got the highest score on the machine. I felt unbeatable. Like I had the Midas touch and everything I touched turned to gold. It was a big change to the usual feeling of everything I touched becoming dirty and contaminated.

We spent the night walking around town, swinging around lampposts and giggling at nothing. Everything looked different with acid—it was like we'd found a portal into a parallel new-and-improved version of the world, where things were almost the exact same just a shinier and happier version.

That was the start of acid for me. I fell in love with the drug and couldn't get enough of it. It was fairly cheap and the lads from Phibsboro gave us plenty of freebies too. After a while, one tab a night turned into two, which turned into five, and before I knew it I was popping them like Tic Tacs and losing count.

It wasn't all fun and games though. The comedown could be horrible. You could go into the horrors altogether and get very paranoid. And the more highs you had, the worse the paranoia got. Everyone was looking at me and everyone was talking about me. At least that's what I thought. But acid numbed the pain in my head for a little while at least and the paranoia was worth that short bit of relief.

*

I dropped out of school altogether during the Inter Cert year. I did the exam all right and I scraped a pass but after that I just wanted out. I made up some excuse about wanting to train as a hairdresser and how I'd managed to line up a job. Of course, this was complete fabrication on my part. I was the girl who ran a mile in the opposite direction if I saw a loose strand of hair. But I left anyway and that marked the end of my school days.

It was around this time that I stopped vomiting in the mornings too. I'm not sure why this was. Maybe it had to do with me being old enough to be able to get out of the house more. I also now had drink and drugs to take away the pain and sickness. All my other routines stayed the same though. I still had my Rice Krispies, my bowl and spoon, the orange juice and the pill. And by the afternoon, I'd be passed out on the couch as usual from tiredness. Even though Da wasn't calling to my room at night anymore, I'd still feel anxiety taking over my body every evening as the sun went down. I couldn't control it. And then there were the nightmares. Sleep was a double-edged sword—although I badly needed the rest, it meant making myself vulnerable to nightmares.

Da continued to spy on me but I did what I could to hide from him. I'd turn the light off before getting undressed or get undressed under my dressing gown. I even tried using my Ma and Da's en suite, but Da wised up and bored holes under the sink that allowed him to spy on the whole bathroom. All he had to do was open the door of the hot-press, get down on his knees and peer through. I often stuffed newspapers into the holes just so he knew that I knew. But it didn't bother him at all. He just pulled them out and carried on watching. He didn't care that I knew.

Chapter Eight

The first job I ever had was in Burgerland on O'Connell Street. I pretended to my ma that the hairdressing job had fallen through. I was glad to be out of the house.

I loved the job in Burgerland. The staff came from all different walks of life: there were college students, college dropouts, kids like me who had dropped out of school and others who were in it for the long haul and wanted to become a manager one day. I didn't care what anyone had been doing before they ended up in Burgerland 'cause once they put on the uniform we were all on the same level and we all followed the same rules. In between the hard work, we had the best of craic and many of the people became friends first and co-workers second.

Every Sunday at Burgerland, I was given the role of dressing up as a packet of fries in a big foam costume. I had to go out on to the street and shake hands with passing kids, who either ran away from me in fear or fell at my feet in adoration. Most of the other staff refused to do this job, mainly because they'd have felt like a prat. The foam costume reminded me a little of the Fozzy Bear one I had worn in the Gaiety. No one could see me. I could hide behind a screen and be someone else for a while. So I volunteered for the role as the hideous sponge packet of fries and I'd dare anyone else to show as much enthusiasm for it as I did.

When I was working the early shifts in Burgerland I used to get a lift into town with one of the managers who lived near me in Castleknock. Things at home were a bit better by then 'cause Da, who was forever changing jobs, was working in England. He was away from Monday to Friday and then I'd be gone out all weekend between work and partying so I hardly saw him at all.

I used to tell my manager that Da lived in England. I don't know why I lied—I guess it was the reality I secretly wanted. But one morning my manager called to the door for me when Da was home and he answered it. Afterwards, in the car on the way into work, my manager asked me about him. I felt terrible being caught out on this lie. I just muttered something about him being back for a while and he didn't ask me any more questions. But that morning I realised that if I didn't get this shit sorted in my head that I'd ruin the little life I'd built up for myself by telling silly lies. So, feeling like I was now safe from my da, I started blocking things out. One by one I pushed the bad memories to the back of my mind, well out of reach.

The Burgerland Christmas do the following year was a great night out. Temporary staff were brought in so that we could all go to the party. The function was held in a city-centre hotel and after we had gotten the meal out of the way the disco started and the real fun began.

I was in the middle of tearing up the dance floor when, out of the corner of my eye, I saw a cute guy walking in. He was obviously into mod music judging by his skin-tight haircut. I asked one of my co-workers who he was and she told me he was the brother of one of the supervisors in another Burgerland branch. Deadly.

I got on great with this supervisor and we were always buzzing off of one another. So, you know how you are at 16, you find out if he's single, does he like the look of you and so on. After the usual intervention by a friend, who sidles up to the guy, giggles and whispers, 'My mate fancies you', he came over and asked me to dance. His name was *Billy* and we clicked straight away.

After the party, a gang of us went back to *Billy's* house where myself and *Billy* cosied up together on the sofa, surrounded by all the other newly formed couples, who were kissing and whispering sweet nothings into each other's ears.

Billy told me he was 17 years old. He had left school early like me but he had landed on his feet with a good job in a printers. He had a lovely sensitive side to him that came to light the more I talked to him.

I went into work the next day walking on air. I was dying to hear from him. A few days went by with no word and I was climbing the walls but then he turned up in Burgerland one day with a mate of his. I remember overhearing his friend saying, 'She's lovely man!' I was especially pleased 'cause I was wearing the not-so-flattering Burgerland uniform, complete with a red cap and hair net.

Myself and *Billy* were practically inseparable from that day on. I was besotted. That Christmas, he bought me a silver Claddagh ring but I'd only had it a few days when I lost it somewhere in my bedroom. I'm not very religious but the ring meant so much to me that I got down on both knees and said a prayer to my namesake saint. My full name is Audrey Jude Delaney and Saint Jude is the patron saint of hopeless cases. I have to laugh sometimes at how apt my naming was. I prayed until I had carpet burns on my two knees from all the kneeling. But it worked. The ring turned up in the most unlikely of places and I found my faith in God being gradually restored.

Over the next few weeks, *Billy* and I ran up ferocious phone bills between us. We just couldn't bear to be apart so the minute we separated and returned to our own homes, we'd be on the phone to one another. I would go down to the phone box across from the shop in my estate and he would ring it at a pre-arranged time.

I'd go down in the lashing rain or gale-force winds just to talk to him, even if we'd already spent the last few days living in each other's pocket. There were no mobile phones back then. I lived two bus journeys away from Billy but whenever I visited him, either his brother or his da always insisted on giving me a lift home. He had a lovely family and they all treated me like I was one of their own.

*

Drugs were becoming a big problem for me around the time *Billy* and I got together. I never told him about it but

I took whatever I could whenever I could. I was taking hash, acid and uppers and downers in the form of pills. I also took other tablets that I think were Valium but I never knew for sure. All these pills were cheap; kids as young as 14 sold them for pocket money. I took anything offered to me really; half of the pills could have just been antibiotics for all I knew. I just took whatever was going and hoped for a high.

One night though, I was in a right bitch of a mood because I had nothing to take. I had been spending so much time with *Billy* that I had lost contact with the people who usually hooked me up. So that night myself and *Billy* went to see a band in this club in Dublin. I felt all grown-up because the last time I'd been in the club had been seven years earlier for a roller-disco night. The band sang the song 'My Girl' that night and this became mine and *Billy*'s song from then on. After the band, *Billy* wanted to go to his friend's 16th birthday party. It was taking place in a shed at the back of the guy's house where music could be blared as loud as they wanted. But a half an hour into the party I got all stroppy when I realised that no one had any alcohol.

'Jesus, is this it? It's like a kid's disco,' I said to *Billy*.

'It's just getting started. It'll probably warm up in a few minutes.'

'But sure no one has brought drink or anything. How can you get a buzz going? This is boring.'

I didn't say what I was really thinking, 'Where are the bleedin' drugs?'

Looking back, I'm mortified by how I acted but I think I just panicked at the thought of having to meet all these new people completely sober. I'd have no choice but to be me. And the problem was that I didn't like me.

'*Billy*, can we leave? I don't know anyone and the girls are looking me up and down and making me feel uncomfortable.'

'C'mon, lets go so.'

So we left and headed to a nearby pub. I downed several vodkas one after another until the room was spinning but at least my thoughts weren't going at 90 miles an hour anymore.

*

The following April, after *Billy* and I had been together for four months, the inevitable conversation about sex came up. I knew I definitely loved him by now. He was a massive part of my life and I was sure that he felt the same about me. I was always staying over in his house, sleeping in his sister's room. But every so often we'd get the house all to ourselves and we'd climb into his bed and kiss and cuddle.

Billy treated me like an angel. He was the only guy I'd ever been with who made me feel special. There was nothing he wouldn't do for me and he always put me first. The only thing that confused me was how come he didn't see the dirt in me.

Fear stopped us going all the way for the first couple of months. I was 16 and a half and I was mad about *Billy* but I found it all very confusing. My biggest fear was that he'd be able to tell that something had gone on before him. But lust won out in the end and we arranged to do it down by the Phoenix Park one day. It was all very mechanical. There was no such thing as foreplay; *Billy* kissed me for a few seconds before putting on a condom. We knew nothing about STDs but we were definitely scared of pregnancy. He came quickly. Afterwards, as we were getting dressed, *Billy* turned to me and said, 'I thought you were supposed to bleed the first time.'

My face turned scarlet. *Billy* was a gentle soul and he wasn't saying this in an accusing way, he just seemed confused.

I panicked and within days I'd finished with him. I just couldn't handle the sexual side of the relationship. I hated lying to him and I was so bad at it that I was convinced he believed he wasn't my first. The sex reminded me of my da too and I worried that now that we had done it once, I'd have to do it all the time. The only way to stop the bad memories coming flooding back was to finish with *Billy*. So I pulled the plug on my relationship with the loveliest bloke I had ever met. I was heartbroken but I desperately needed to feel in control again.

After we broke up, I started hanging around with my old friends on the north side of Dublin again. I got more and more heavily into drugs. I started dating unsavoury types, simply because they liked the same thing as me—drugs. We smoked hash, popped pills and drank and drank. I still had a bit of a head on my shoulders but being out of it meant you didn't have to think, feel or answer awkward questions. I had become very adept at blocking out the abuse, even to the point where I was able to have sexual relationships without thinking of my da. When I was 17, I got engaged to a guy who Da didn't approve of. This made it all the more interesting, but it wasn't to last. It was just another way of rebelling as far as I was concerned.

I didn't carry the emotions of the past with these sexual experiences, because at this stage I had almost forgotten my past. I didn't remember anymore; I had pushed it out of my head. I still had the emptiness, the pain, and the mental torture that I couldn't explain. But drinking and taking drugs solved that one for me. They allowed me to function for a while.

*

I decided to leave Burgerland when I was still 16. After listening to all the students there going on about their studies, I realised they had a future and I didn't. I loved working there and part of me hated leaving but I knew I had to do something with my life.

I enrolled in a full-time IT course with Anco on the Jamestown Road in Finglas. Computers were just getting popular around that time. I learned word processing, electronics and programming. It was all very new to me though and to be honest I hadn't a clue about what I was doing. I sat in on the electronics class all right but most of it went over my head. I loved the word processing though.

That course was one of the best things I ever did and it certainly stood to me in the future. You got a small training fee for attending too—it wasn't a full wage but it was enough to get by on. I used the money to go on and do an evening typing class. I put a lot of effort into the typing and bought myself a heavy steel typewriter to practise on in the evenings. So during the week I focused on my studies and at the weekends I let my hair down and went mad.

I was still trying to block out memories of the abuse but the more I did this the more emotional and angry I got. When I wasn't practising for my course, I was out of my head on drugs.

I thought that I had managed to put all the abuse behind me and I was now a normal, functioning young adult who had taken charge of her life. The demons were never too far away, though, and my mask would slip when I least expected it.

One of my supervisors in the course asked me several times if I was all right, or if I needed to talk. I had no idea why he was asking me this. Was he referring to the way I sometimes cried in front of people in the class? Or did he notice how out of it I sometimes was? I always had a made-up story at hand to justify my tears. But then more questions were asked and cracks would begin to appear in my story. The supervisor was genuinely concerned. But I didn't even know what was wrong with me myself, so how could I tell him.

I was just trying to lose myself in my relationships so that I wouldn't have to face up to my own problems.

By now I had pushed everything that happened with Da so far to the back of my mind that it was like I no longer had a past. I had blanked it all out. I still had the empty feeling I could never explain but drink and drugs solved that one for me. So long as I had a constant supply of both, I could function.

*

I finished up my typing course and got a job as a receptionist in a gym on Eden Quay in Dublin. I was naturally well-mannered and polite so customer service came easy to me. I took the job very seriously and I found myself plunged into a completely different world to the one I had previously been living in. The gym attracted people from all walks of life. You had shop assistants, students, guards, builders, solicitors, doctors, professors—a whole cross-section of society. But when people got changed into their gym gear, they all looked the very same to me.

I discovered that I was excellent at sales and it wasn't long before I was earning good commission on top of a decent wage. Slowly but surely, my lifestyle was changing. I started socialising with people from work and I found that it was nice to have nights out that didn't involve drugs. It made me realise that I'd had enough of them. Before I'd started working in the gym, I'd used drugs the whole time.

Around the same time, my manager *Joseph* used to walk me to the bus stop every evening. Maybe it was the chivalry and the fact that I was feeling so vulnerable at the time but I found myself developing feelings for him. It was a very physical attraction. He would only have to walk by me in the corridor and sparks would fly. He made it clear that he felt the same way and we went on a few dates.

all my fault

*

But I spent my early twenties feeling exposed and raw. I felt like the bubbly me that I'd once been able to present to the world was fading away and now my dark inner feelings were on show.

Around this time, a friend of mine told me she was depressed and was going to see a psychiatrist. My overwhelming feeling was one of jealousy, which might sound strange. I was jealous that someone could go inside her head and fix it. I wished so badly that I could get someone to do that for me. I didn't know how to go about it, though, and I was too embarrassed to ask my friend. I thought it would be so simple. A quack would show you a few blobs on the page, you would tell him what you thought of it, and he would ask you some more questions, maybe hypnotise you. Then he would make a diagnosis and you would be cured.

But I was far from cured. In reality, I became agoraphobic. Without realising it, a desperation to hide away from the world crept up on me and I found myself withdrawing into a shell once more. I stopped seeing my friends and family. The black thoughts had taken over. The louder the thoughts became, the more I turned to drugs to quieten them. I had gotten to the stage where alcohol alone wasn't enough to take the pain away. It was just the appetiser before the real tranquilliser. So I used my contacts to get my hands on whatever I could—hash, ecstasy, speed, coke. I smoked heroin too but I stopped short of doing it the dirty way, as I called it, which was using it intravenously. I used anything I could get my hands on to escape my thoughts.

I never felt like I was a junkie though. I was an addict all right but I still had my principles. I never slept with anyone to get money for drugs, never robbed to get them and never got behind the wheel of a car with drugs in my system. So to this day, I always say that I wasn't a 'junkie junkie' – just a junkie. It's my own personal thin line maybe—but it makes me feel better.

Chapter Nine

I fell for *Joseph*, my manager in the gym, in a big way. I'd only been seeing *Joseph* a short while when our relationship was tested by an emotional rollercoaster. I found out that my beloved ex-boyfriend *Billy* had been killed in a crash. He'd been riding his mod scooter with a friend when a van came crashing into them. His neck was broken and he died instantly.

Billy's sister rang me at work to tell me the bad news and when I hung up the phone my body was like jelly I was shaking so much. *Billy* had been my first love and I'd never stopped loving him—I just hadn't been able for the sexual side of the relationship at the time. So I'd tucked my feelings for him away in a corner of my heart and broke it off thinking I was saving myself from future heartbreak.

Joseph drove me to the funeral. He must have suspected that I still had feelings for my dear lost *Billy* but he never once asked me any questions. He just held my hand throughout and let me know I wasn't alone.

Billy's family welcomed me with open arms. They even took me in the head funeral car and we all just held one another and bawled our eyes out.

The church was thronged. People were spilling out on to the streets. I cried and I cried throughout the funeral ceremony. I couldn't imagine how terrible his parents must have been feeling if I felt this bad. They played 'My Girl' during the Mass—mine and *Billy's* song—and that just made the waterworks ten times worse.

I lost days after the funeral. I couldn't work; I couldn't eat; I couldn't sleep. I just wandered around in a confused daze, remembering all the good times I'd had with *Billy* and hating myself for screwing it all up in the end.

I blamed myself.

Da didn't figure in the equation at all 'cause at this stage I was still blocking the abuse out. I didn't have a past as far as I was concerned.

My life had been all over the place the last few months. Between changing jobs, *Billy* dying and meeting *Joseph*. The only constant in all of this was the empty feeling that just wouldn't go away. There was something wrong with me. I knew that much for sure. I was different. I just didn't know how. I started getting flashbacks of my childhood. Although I was fairly good at suppressing the memories, I've learnt that you can't bury them forever.

After *Billy's* funeral, *Joseph* became the glue holding me together. My feelings for him grew stronger the more I got to know him. He was 26 and had recently separated from his wife, with whom he had two little girls. When Da heard this he went mental and I had to listen to lectures on what a disgrace I was for dating a married man. He even got *Joseph* on his own one evening and tried to convince him to walk away from me. And it wasn't just Da who disagreed with the relationship—some of my friends had their tuppence worth to give too. Eventually, me and *Joseph* became an official couple against the wishes of everyone. I even had to leave my job in the gym.

*

One day when I was working in an office, I had a severe attack of flashbacks. I felt my throat tighten. I couldn't deal with it. At lunchtime when no one was around, I rang the Rape Crisis Centre, asking if I could speak to someone in confidence. The person who answered the phone put me on hold for a moment, and then asked if I could give them a number so they could ring me back. Like I was gonna! I didn't even know what to say. I just hung up and pushed it out of my mind for years, blocking it out again.

I drifted from job to job after that, trying to find somewhere I could grow some roots. The one thing I knew I was good at though—no matter what the area—was sales. So myself and *Joseph* decided to combine our skills. He was a world-class power lifter and a fabricator by trade, with a sideline in making gym equipment for other businesses, I was great at sales and we both had experience in the gym industry, so why not try and open up our own gym? We had loads of clients between us who liked us and who we knew would follow us. All we needed was some business smarts and someone to help with the finances. *Joseph* thought that it would be a great idea to get Da involved in it. He thought it would help build some bridges between the two of them and also Da would obviously provide the missing business acumen. I didn't like the idea but I had no good reason to give *Joseph*. I had no good reason to give myself. So it all went ahead. We took out loans and started up a toning table and beauty salon in Lucan in west Dublin. Around the same time we opened the business, *Joseph* and I bought a house in Celbridge in County Kildare. It was a good-size, red-brick bungalow with a large garden. But it was the two dogs we got rather than the house that had me excited. We got a Greyhound/Labrador cross-breed who I named Frisky, after a horse I'd once backed that had won big, and a small hairy Terrier cross who I named Peanut. He was the liveliest and funniest dog I ever saw. The dogs completed the house for me—it felt like we were one big happy family. All that was missing was the white-picket fence.

When the centre first opened, *Joseph* got me an old mustard-coloured Allegro car. He had it sprayed pink and gave it to me as a present. I had never had a driving lesson in my life. The only driving I had ever done was sitting behind the wheel of cars robbed by my mates or else 'borrowed' from someone's Ma or Da. But I loved driving. Doing handbrake turns and donuts in quiet open areas was the best buzz ever. I'm not proud of these things now but at the time I didn't understand what other people got so worked up about. To me, it was an adrenalin rush and a bit of fun. I was the only girl brave enough to get involved in the driving side of things; the other girls just sat in the back and came along for the spin.

A couple of weeks after *Joseph* presented me with the car, we had one of our first big rows. I can't remember what it was about now, I just remember the great escape the car allowed me. I had just gotten my provisional license and paid the insurance and I couldn't get out of the house fast enough. I jumped into my pink Allegro and off I went. I could speed away from all my troubles just like that. It was a great feeling. Like the costume I wore in the pantomime or the Burgerland fries costume, the car allowed me to hide from people. I had a windscreen to shield me. I could just whiz by people and get to where I wanted to go without having to stop and talk and risk them catching a glimpse of my dirty soul.

*

Even though me and *Joseph* were playing happy families, I hadn't abandoned my peculiar morning rituals. I still got up every morning and fetched my bowl and spoon, poured the cereal, and stirred and ate it in the exact same manner as I'd been doing since I was a child. I couldn't leave the house if this ritual hadn't been followed to perfection. Joseph found it a little strange and he used to joke about it with his mates but I think in a way he found it a little endearing.

My health was also as up and down as always and the crazy hours I was working in the gym weren't helping matters. I worked 12-hour days. I was admitted to hospital at one stage with a painful, icy feeling in my left arm. The doctors told me that the stress of my job was tiring out my heart. They took me off the pill and told me to cut back on work but things were just starting to take off so there was no chance of that. I didn't pay too much attention anyway. Aches and pains, doctors and nurses—they had all become like wallpaper in my life to the point that I no longer took much notice of them. I was already hooked on medicines at this stage, both prescribed and illegal. I needed Valium on a regular basis and also continued to take sleeping pills. It was the only way I could hope to get any sleep at night. Taking tablets and medication had also become part of my daily routine, and it would take many years before I even tried to address this problem.

I also started getting major migraines around this time that seemed to coincide with Da being present. The minute he walked into the same room as me, I tensed up. The pressure inside my head was terrible. I hated him being around. I found the way he acted around women humiliating; the way he leered at them and used any excuse to be all touchy-feely.

I remember one day Da and *Joseph* were in the office discussing something. I just nipped in for a second to grab something from one of the cupboards when this overwhelming wave of emotions washed over me. It was like all the feelings I'd been trying to quash got swept into a tornado and it was now bulldozing through me at break-neck speed. I don't know how else to describe it. Black thoughts had come dislodged in my head. I tried to push them to the back of my mind but next thing I knew everything went black. I had fainted. I had fallen flat on my face in front of Da and *Joseph*. When I came to, I told them I'd been feeling a little dizzy but it was nothing to worry about.

*

It didn't take long for cracks to appear in mine and *Joseph*'s relationship. I still loved him and knew he loved me, but we started rowing a lot.

In the beginning, we had the sweetest relationship ever, but in time things started to go wrong between us. It was no one's fault; it was just something that happened.

So our home life was missing a lot more than the white-picket fence by now. But I kept telling myself it was nothing I couldn't handle. And if things ever did get to be too much, sure I could always just call up a mate and get them to hook me up with something to get me out of my head.

After our first year in business, we were doing well so we decided to extend the gym using equipment *Joseph* had been working on. We added a sauna and showers to the works, so now we had the toning tables, a beauty salon and a mixed gym.

In our third year, the interest rates on mortgages and loans doubled and we got hit badly. Money was tight everywhere and the clients had to put their own priorities first; their gym membership was way down their list of concerns. So we started losing customers fast. Our loans were outstanding and our own mortgage on the house in Celbridge went through the roof.

It was all coming tumbling down.

We were in the middle of a financial crisis and we were all financially exposed. It got to the stage where we had no choice but to liquidate the gym. We were completely broke. We just about had a roof over our heads but the electricity in the house had been cut off and we didn't even have any heating.

The pressure on us was overwhelming. I tried everything to escape from reality. When *Joseph* went out with friends, I usually took the dogs with me for company and escaped to my car. I'd put the radio on full blast just so I wouldn't be able to hear my own thoughts; whispering voices that spread like smoke in my mind and threatened to blot out everything if I turned off the music and listened to what they had to say.

For most of my life, everyone had thought of me as smiley, bubbly, happy-go-lucky Audrey. Nobody knew the real me. On the outside, I had a great sense of humour and I loved a laugh. But the sadness was always lurking on the inside, threatening to brim over and spoil everything. I used to think that the happy me the rest of the world saw was just a lie and not the real me. But I now know that it was the sad, confused and empty me that should never have existed. During my late teens and early adulthood, any real happiness I felt had to be drug induced. I couldn't fall asleep without taking pills and when I did finally nod off, I would be hopping all over the bed with nightmares. I'd never remember the details of the dreams the next morning but I'd be left with a horrible feeling in the pit of my stomach.

It was after yet another row with *Joseph* that I was sitting in my little pink haven one day with the radio blaring. The music faded and the news came on. The newsreader was going through all the top stories and I remember her saying the words 'child abuse'. I froze. Every bone in my body tensed up and I felt my fists clenching involuntarily. The words had struck a cord with me. I tried to push them out of my mind and pretend I hadn't heard them. But it was too late. A door had been reopened somewhere in my mind—one that I had sealed shut a very long time ago.

Once this door opened, it seemed I lost control of my memories. Whereas I was once able to block them out, now they assaulted me on a daily basis. Everywhere I turned the word 'child abuse' kept popping up. I heard about priests, fathers, uncles. It seemed to be everywhere. I'm not sure if this was a new thing or if it was just registering with me for the first time—I honestly don't know. But I slowly acknowledged what this phrase 'child abuse' meant. Then I absorbed the words 'child sexual abuse.' This was overpowering. I couldn't deal with it and I went into a state of denial.

*

After we lost the gym, I was in and out of jobs for a long time, unable to hold anything down for very long. I felt like, to add to all my other problems, I now had no sense of purpose. Nightmares, migraines, flashbacks, money troubles. It was like a twisted funfair ride that just went round and round in circles and I couldn't make it stop. My problems were like a disease that had invaded my body and there was no cure for it. I was convinced it was terminal so what was the point in living? It was time to take action.

So not for the first time in my life, I made a pathetic attempt to end it all. I bought some alcohol and drank until my senses were nicely numbed. I took a knife that I used as a potato peeler and I began cutting into my skin. It didn't do much damage so I replaced it with a serrated bread knife. I couldn't press it down hard enough though. Both arms were left with mere skin abrasions. This wasn't the first time I had tried to slit my wrists. I had made a feeble attempt before. But it was the same scenario. I was left with a few scratches—silly looking slices on my wrists mocking me for being too chicken to go deeper. Then I heard the dogs barking and it dawned on me; if I died who would feed the dogs? It was a silly thing to focus on but it brought me back to my senses. Here I was again, several years later and the only thing that had changed was that things had gotten worse.

I spent the next two weeks getting as out of my head as I possibly could. I had hit rock bottom. I knew I couldn't sink much lower. I had barely enough money to buy food never mind keep me stocked up on ecstasy and alcohol. You could say that they took over my world. If it wasn't alcohol it was drugs. I couldn't have a drink without a line of cocaine. I became dependent on anything I could get my hands on, simply to live with myself. I was the worst company for myself and I was in a very lonely place.

I felt exposed and raw. Could everyone see how crazy I had become? I became even more agoraphobic and I withdrew from the world. I was all alone in a very dark and lonely room and I desperately needed to grasp someone's hand in the dark if I was going to make it out of there alive.

So I decided to do the unthinkable. I don't know where I found the courage but I sat down and started writing a letter to *Joseph*. I told him all about the abuse. I just wrote down everything that came into my head. I'm not sure how much sense it made. But I told him about the years of abuse at the hands of Da in the most basic language I could. The pages were soaking from my tears and the ink was running down the page by the time I had finished writing.

Joseph was away that evening so when I had finished writing the letter I ran out to a phone box. I dialled his number, my hands shaking so bad I could barely hold the receiver.

'*Joseph*,' I said, 'I need you to come home.'

I had never told him what to do before so he listened carefully, instinctively knowing something serious was up.

'Don't come into the sitting room when you get back. Go into the kitchen and read the letter I've written to you and then come in to me in the sitting room.'

I hung up and went back to the house. I was terrified. How would he react? Would he shout and give out to me? Tell me it was my fault?

All I could do now was wait.

An hour later, I heard the dreaded sound of his key in the door.

'Audrey, where are you?'

'Just do what I told you. I can't talk to you until you do,' I shouted back tearfully.

While he was reading the letter, I couldn't stop dry retching. I hadn't eaten in days.

'I'm shocked,' *Joseph* said when he came into the sitting room. 'I certainly wasn't expecting this.'

I didn't know what to say next. He took me in his arms, which was exactly what I needed from him, and we spent the night crying and talking. It's the first time I remember crying for myself and feeling sorry for myself. I felt so vulnerable.

Not only had I opened a door to my past but I had also allowed somebody else to step into it with me. I could hear the little girl inside me thanking me for finally listening to her cries. I heard the sweet voice I had heard in my bedroom all those years ago, and I recognised it instantly. But the adult me was terrified and kept asking if I had done the right thing.

I didn't know what we were going to do next. When I say 'we', I mean me and *Joseph* because I felt that by telling him everything I had somehow won the old *Joseph* back and we were a team again. All our past differences would fade away. He would understand everything and it would be his goal to make things right for me. I had a sense of belief for the first time in my life about what partnership really means.

At first, *Joseph* wanted to kill Da. He even made for the door a few times, saying he was off to find him, but he never got any further. I didn't want Da dead though. I wanted answers. I wanted huge gaping holes in my memory filled in. I wanted to know if someone had abused Da when he was a child and if it had been a case of history repeating itself. But all I really wanted at the end of the day was for someone to hug me and make all the pain go away.

I wanted that so much. I deserved so much.

Behind *Joseph*'s anger, I think there was also a sense of relief. He now knew there was a reason for the way I had acted over the years. That was it. Problem solved. We would sort out my issues with the past and then we'd get a happy-ever-after ending to our relationship.

'This is what we'll do,' was *Joseph*'s favourite sentence over the next few weeks as we mulled it over in our minds.

But I still hadn't said the words 'My da sexually abused me' out loud yet. I had written them down on a piece of paper. And I wasn't sure if I was ready for the next step. I wasn't sure if I was ready to swing the door on the past wide open just yet.

Chapter Ten

After a few weeks of talking things over till there were no words left to say, *Joseph* suggested that we should share the massive burden we'd been carrying with someone else. He insisted on bringing my brother *Mark* into the picture. In the end, I hadn't much choice but to agree. I knew that there was no talking *Joseph* out of it. But I also knew in my heart that it was time. I couldn't hold it all in anymore—the pain in my gut, the guilt, the sense of shame. The longer I kept this secret, the more I felt my head swelling with the pressure of it all. I needed to let it all out before it killed me. I needed help. I had to tell the boys and my mother. Surely Ma would be able to help.

So we decided to tell *Mark* first. When I say we, it was really *Joseph* who would be doing all the telling. I still couldn't vocalise any of it. So it was arranged that *Joseph* and *Mark* would meet for a drink, while I stayed at home, drinking on my own. Again, waiting for the key to turn in the lock. It felt like I had spent my whole life waiting.

I was so frightened that *Mark* would be angry with me; that he wouldn't believe me—or even worse, that he would blame me. I need not have worried. When the two of them came home, *Mark* walked right up to me and gave me a big hug.

'Jesus Audrey, why didn't you tell me sooner?' he said.

He seemed shocked but who could blame him after hearing that news?

'We have to tell Ma,' he said.

'I want to but I'm not sure if I have the nerve. I need you to help me.'

Mark was very understanding.

'It's all clicking into place for me now Audrey. The memories. Da calling into your room every night, him spending ages up in the attic. It all makes sense now.'

'I'm just so glad that you believe me and that I don't have to prove anything to you.'

I had dropped the bomb and I knew there was no going back now. I just felt so scared—scared of the unknown. I wasn't sure if I was ready for the next hurdle—telling the rest of the family. I felt overwhelmed by shame and responsibility; I didn't want to hurt them and shatter their world with this revelation. I couldn't stop thinking about Ma and my brothers. Was I right in doing this to them? Would I not be better just to keep my mouth shut and spare them the pain?

I felt like I was losing control. Everything was moving too fast.

My little brother *Dan* was celebrating his 21st in two weeks' time so myself, *Joseph* and *Mark* decided we would let him celebrate in peace before we dropped the bombshell. We didn't want to spoil his party. I had to make up an excuse to get out of going to his party. I felt so bad but I just couldn't face everyone. Over the last few years, as the memories had begun trickling back, I'd avoided Da as much as possible, and at this point I would have been happy to never lay eyes on him again.

My little brother's 21st came and went. He was gutted I didn't go and I hated not telling him the truth but I knew it was for his own good. I left it about a week after the party before ringing up Ma.

'Hiya Ma. It's me. Audrey.'

'Are you all right love? I haven't heard from you in ages. You're not sick are you?'

I think Ma was convinced that after all the years I'd spent going in and out of hospital, that the doctors had finally found something terribly wrong with me.

'No Ma. I'm not sick. But I've been having problems that I can't talk about over the phone. Can you come up and see me?' I asked.

'Is it serious? Can you not tell me over the phone? I'll be out of me mind with worry otherwise.'

'No Ma, I have to say this to your face. It's not something to be talked about on the phone.'

Ma agreed to come up later that night. *Mark* drove her over to Celbridge and then he and *Joseph* went for drinks, leaving us to it.

I sat across from her in the sitting room, with a bottle of wine by my side for Dutch courage and a second one chilling in the fridge as back-up. I wrung my hands nervously for about ten minutes while I tried to say the words aloud. Ma sat staring at me, her face looking anxious, tired and drawn.

'Ma,' I finally said, 'Da abused me . . . sexually.'

Ma didn't say anything for a minute or two. It was like she was trying to digest what I had said and make sense of it. Then, slowly, every last drop of colour began to drain from her face.

'When? Where?' she cried. 'How come I never knew? When did he do it?'

'Lots of times, Ma. I don't remember when it first happened it was so long ago now. I was only small.'

'Why didn't you tell me?'

'I don't know. I . . . I don't know. 'Cause it was always there. I didn't know it was wrong at first and by the time I did, I was too scared and I didn't want to hurt you.'

I started rambling, grappling in the dark for excuses that would put an end to her never-ending list of questions. But I didn't have a one-sentence answer for her. It wasn't that simple.

The phone suddenly rang and interrupted our conversation. I knew straight away it was Da.

'Yeah she's okay,' said Ma, 'I can't talk to you right now. I'll talk to you tomorrow. Your dinner is in the fridge so just take it out and heat it up.'

I wondered did Da suspect the game was up? Or did he think that I had been diagnosed with some terrible illness and that was why I had been so desperate to talk to Ma?

'I never knew,' continued Ma when she had hung up on

128

Da. Ma didn't need to tell me this. I knew she had never known, never suspected.

Joseph and *Mark* came back from the pub a few hours later. By this stage, my head was spinning from a mixture of the drink and all the crying, so I don't really remember what exactly happened next. I felt so terribly sad. I had never seen Ma cry before, and I couldn't bear to see her so upset. I know a conversation took place between *Mark*, *Joseph* and Ma, but I don't remember what we decided to do next.

The next day I begged Ma not to go. I needed her to hold me and somehow make it all better. She stayed one more night and when she was leaving the next day, she said to me, 'I have to ask your da to his face. I need to say it to him.'

It wasn't that she didn't believe me, she insisted, she just needed to hear him say it. *Mark* brought her home and stood right behind her when she confronted Da. I was told afterwards that Ma had asked Da straight out if he'd abused me.

'No . . . I mean yeah . . . I think so,' Da responded. And then after a long pause, '. . . maybe once or twice. I can't really remember.'

That was all Ma needed to hear. Da left the house that night. He went quietly—like a scared rabbit—probably hoping and praying that everyone would soon calm down and he'd be back home before long. When he'd packed his bags and left, Ma and *Mark* sat *Fergus* and *Dan* down and told them everything. They said they weren't surprised once they had been told what had happened. It was like they'd been given the last piece of a jigsaw puzzle and suddenly everything made sense. Da hanging around in my room every night.

The night my brothers were told, I called over to the house to see them. I had to make sure they were okay. My heart ached for them. I didn't want to cause them any pain. We all ended up crying, hugging and drinking into the early hours of the morning. Not one of them doubted what I had said, and I was so grateful for this. Everyone immediately accepted it as true, and it was so important for me to hear this. My brothers said that they hadn't realised it but they had been holding their stomachs in for years and now that everything was out in the open it was like they could breathe again. The only problem was that the air was full of pollutants that half choked you with every breath.

Da rented a room in a house a couple of miles away from Castleknock. He tried to get in contact with me and my brothers, either by writing us letters or sending requests via Ma. I wasn't having any of it though. I have no idea what thoughts were going through his head at this point. I'm sure he was feeling sorry for himself and worrying about what would happen next. I doubt he ever expected it to go much further.

The Christmas season arrived when we were in the midst of all this hurt and anger. We celebrated it without Da, with a sense of dirt and shame hanging over us in place of the Christmas decorations. The festive season just seemed to highlight the black hole we'd been wallowing in.

We didn't know where to go from here. Someone

suggested that the Rape Crisis Centre might be able to offer me some advice, so I made the call. I have heard loads of stories from other people about the great work this centre does, and I would encourage others to use it, but in my case I felt like I was more confused by the end of it all.

With me floundering, *Joseph* took it upon himself to decide what we should do next, but losing control had been my biggest fear all along. I didn't want to be pushed into making a decision I didn't feel ready for.

The tension simmered over to boiling point and a lot of fights broke out. I felt like the situation was of my own making in a way and yet I felt I didn't have any control over it anymore. Ma tried hard to make things right, but it was beyond her control.

About four months after Ma first confronted Da and he moved out, he decided to return home.

This prompted my brothers to leave the house straight away. They slept on sofas and floors in mates' houses as none of them had the money to pay deposits on houses.

So Da was back.

I couldn't believe it. I didn't want to believe it. I felt so worthless and felt that he was getting the upper hand.

When Da moved back into the house in Castleknock, he contacted a counsellor who dealt with sexual abusers.

Ma then paid for me to see a counsellor. My counsellor was a nice woman but I wasn't yet ready to confront my past so I got fuck all out of it. Except for the inconvenience of having to travel all the way from Celbridge to the south side. I'd come home feeling raw.

I never told the counsellor the intimate details of the abuse and in time I started to wonder if it was all worth it. Had I not been better off before I confessed the abuse to anyone? Had Ma and my brothers not been better off too? Maybe if I just pretended everything was okay and that I'd prefer to sweep it all under the carpet, everyone would be able to get on with their lives without this dark cloud hanging over them.

*

I was still in the middle of the counselling when I found out that I was pregnant. It was unplanned but I was delighted. But the counsellor recommended that I stop the sessions. She didn't think it would be good to go too deep into things as the stress of it all could harm the baby. I was happy to stop anyway.

I was very low at this point. I remember I was crossing the road in Celbridge one day when a truck came hurtling around the corner at breakneck speed and for a split second I wanted to step out in front of it and put an end to everything. It would mean my family would be able to close the can of worms I'd opened. The only thing that stopped me that day was my unborn baby. I knew that I had to struggle on for its sake.

At some stage or another, Da's family were told about the abuse. A chosen few were selected and all was revealed to them and them alone. The only member of the family not to be told was Nanny Delaney. It was agreed that at her age the news could kill her.

I loved Nanny dearly and I didn't want to upset her, so I went along with this decision.

None of us had a manual that gave a step-by-step breakdown of what to do. We were all just stumbling along blindly, colliding with walls and doors and all sorts of other obstacles as we tried to find some way out of this situation.

It was arranged that I would go to a meeting with Da's counsellor. Da wouldn't be going, though, as I refused to be in the same room as him.

I didn't find the meeting helpful at all, and I continued to feel hopeless and depressed, more convinced than ever that I should have continued to keep my mouth shut.

*

Back in Celbridge, what had briefly brought me and *Joseph* together was now sending us further apart. We argued non-stop, and as I was the one with the problems, I felt that I was an easy target. The truth was that we were just not compatible.

I suffered with terrible anxiety and it got to the stage where I was barely able to leave the house. Stepping outside in daylight hours gave me the feeling that you get in dreams when you find yourself suddenly standing naked on a street full of people. I just couldn't brave it unless I absolutely had to. I wouldn't go shopping until every last morsel of food in the fridge had been eaten.

Da had hurt me over and over again and would continue to hurt me for the rest of my life. He had admitted to it too.

As far as I was concerned, Da hadn't lost his family—he

had thrown them away. I wasn't responsible for destroying anyone's life; again, Da had done that all by himself. It was all his responsibility.

It was inevitable that my relationship with my mother would be affected by what had happened. For a while, I struggled to keep a relationship of some sorts going with Ma. I'd ring her up but if Da answered my heart would skip a beat and I'd slam the phone back down again. I'd ring back a few minutes later, hoping Ma would pick up the phone on the next ring. We were both caught in this impossible situation.

I just plodded along, feeling more and more angry and hurt all the time. I knew it was only a matter of time before something or someone hit the switch and caused it to boil over.

Around this time, my parents decided to sell the huge house in Castleknock and move to another slightly smaller house nearby. So with the money left over from the sale, Ma gave me and my three brothers a couple of thousand pounds each and told us that it was from her and not Da. She was doing her best to help me.

Nothing could compensate me for what Da had done to me, but because Ma gave it to me, I accepted the money as if it was rightly mine, a kind of early inheritance, and one that wasn't coming from Da. To be honest, I didn't think twice about taking the money. My car at the time was on its last legs so I used the money to buy a new one.

But the money didn't bring me any feelings of justice. I had told my family what happened in order to bring some cleanliness and control into my life, but I still felt sullied, and even worse, I still felt that Da had gotten away with it.

Chapter Eleven

Joseph was delighted when he found out I was pregnant. But within a few weeks, our relationship had gone back to being a struggle. I couldn't stop thinking about how Da had gotten away with everything—his life appeared on the outside to be exactly the same as it was. The only difference now was that he had been exposed as a child abuser to his family. I kept thinking about going to the police and making a complaint, but I'd had some problems already during the pregnancy and the doctors were warning me to take it easy so I certainly didn't feel ready for the gardaí just yet.

My relationship with *Joseph* eventually broke down, and he moved out. Looking back, I guess it was inevitable. The pregnancy was a very lonely time for me. My best friend Mary was the one person who was there for me. She really became a support structure that I clung on to. I really needed someone in my life at that point who just accepted me for who I was, and she provided that and more. I took comfort from having her around and from the feeling of my little baby growing inside of me. I cut out drugs and smoking altogether and my only weakness during the pregnancy was a couple of glasses of wine to help me sleep on the really bad nights.

After we spent time apart, *Joseph* came back for the birth of our son. If I'm truthful, I was glad to have him back, because I was frightened at the thoughts of what lay ahead. When I found out my baby was a boy I thought this might gel us all together.

I can't explain the feeling of complete and utter unconditional love that welled up inside of me when I first laid eyes on my wonderful, gorgeous baby boy who I named Tyrone. I remember lying in bed and feeling his gentle breath on my cheek and with each breath he breathed I suddenly knew the meaning of love and life. It was the most fulfilling emotion I'd ever felt. I had my baby now and nobody was going to take him away from me. I was completely consumed by him. Me and the little man were the only two people who mattered in the world.

Joseph was equally mad about his son, and we tried to make our relationship work. We plodded along happily enough. He adored the baby and he was great with him.

I breastfed Tyrone for about six months after he was born so I didn't go out very much. I didn't mind though. I was happy to spend the weekends with him. I really bonded with Tyrone during this time. I didn't even find it too hard taking care of him on my own. I'd get up to feed him every night and when I'd put him back in his cot, I'd sit and watch him go back to sleep. I just didn't want to take my eyes off him.

When Tyrone was a few months old I started to drink wine in the evenings to help me sleep, as I started having more and more nightmares. This time I remembered the details after I woke up. They were all pretty much the same. Da would sneak into Tyrone's bedroom and steal him from his cot. I couldn't move in the dream so I wasn't able to stop him. I felt so helpless. He'd bring him off and introduce him to little girls and teach him how to humiliate and abuse them. I'd dream that he was taking my son under his wing and trying to pass this disease on to him. My son would fall under his spell. Then the guards would burst in and arrest them both but my baby would get the death sentence while Da would walk free. I'd toss and turn in my bed all night with these bad dreams and when I'd wake in the morning I'd be exhausted and tearful, and the memory of the nightmare would linger for the rest of the day.

*

When Tyrone was one year old, *Joseph* proposed to me. Divorce had been legalised in Ireland so he and his ex-wife were now divorced. We were in a lift in Blanchardstown Shopping Centre, heading down to Dunnes to do some grocery shopping, when he turned to me with a nervous look on his face.

'Will you marry me, like for real, as soon as we can?' he asked.

'Yes,' I stuttered, completely caught off guard. Me and *Joseph* had been up and down and generally all over the place for the last few years but I did love him and I knew

Tyrone needed a father figure in his life. Plus, as an added bonus I would be able to get rid of the name 'Delaney' that I hated. Even though I loved my family, I still couldn't help but associate the name with being dirty and my father.

I had a few drinks with my girlfriends to celebrate the wedding. But, with all the drinking and the craic, things got out of hand during the night and I somehow ended up shaving my head. I loved a bit of craic but it wasn't till the next morning that I realised what I had done. I wouldn't have minded so much only I had the wedding looming. One minute I had long blonde hair down to my bum and the next I had a mousy brown number-two cut. I felt like someone had died when I looked in the mirror the next day and saw my bald head staring back at me.

*

A lot of work went into planning the wedding. The first thing we had to do was make sure that everything was finalised with Joseph's divorce. The divorce law had only recently been passed in this country so the system was still catching up with itself and a lot of paperwork had to be filed.

We decided to get married in England as the registry offices over there were a lot nicer than the ones in Ireland. Since *Joseph* had already been married, a church wedding was not an option. It also helped with my own family situation to go for a minimal wedding. That way I didn't have to worry so much about who knew what and who had to be kept apart from who. It just made life easier.

So just eight weeks after *Joseph* first proposed, we got married in England. Ma, my three brothers and a few close friends came over. Depending on who was asking, I had different excuses for why Da wasn't there.

My dress on the day was floor length and ivory. It wasn't my dream dress but I hadn't any money at the time and wedding dresses cost a small fortune. I looked everywhere for one that I could afford and, eventually, I found a dress in a sale for £100—a bargain.

The ceremony in the registry office was very emotional. *Joseph* even shed a few tears when he saw me and Tyrone walking in. Tyrone looked so cute in a top hat and tails.

We spent the honeymoon in *Joseph*'s Ma's flat in the centre of Bristol. *Joseph* and I spent most of our honeymoon apart from each other, mixing with different people.

It didn't take me long to realise that our wedding wouldn't have a fairytale ending. But at least I knew *Joseph* inside out by now—the good parts and the bad. And that, if nothing else, was a source of comfort.

*

After the wedding, as the months flew by, I found myself getting more and more over-protective of Tyrone. I couldn't bear the thought of anyone harming a hair on his head. I would have killed for him.

At this point I got a book about the subconscious mind—it was all about how to train your mind to think more positively. This started giving me the strength to get through the really bad times.

I started studying different religions and positive thinking, and I formed a technique that had a common denominator with most teachings. My children and I use this technique today. God is at the centre and we train our minds to pray for what we want and we get it. It is full of love and thankfulness, and is non judgemental. It has taken me about eight years to learn about using your subconscious and your soul. But it worked right from the beginning when I started.

The concept made me more determined than ever before to put the pieces of my life back together. And playing happy families with Da was not the way to do that.

I wasn't playing happy families at home with *Joseph* either. Our relationship had started to breakdown once more. When we weren't fighting, our house was deathly quiet which was nearly worse. *Joseph* and I could go for weeks without exchanging any words at all. The only thing that made it bearable was the odd weekend visit from my friend Mary. We would go for a few drinks and have the craic and it reminded me of the life I might have.

It was only when I fell pregnant a second time that I decided I had to leave *Joseph*. My best mate helped me fill the car with clothes, and myself, her and my big belly left the house in Celbridge. The breakup wasn't anyone's fault. The relationship between the two of us just didn't work out.

One of my brothers put me and Tyrone up for a couple of months. I made sure I kept to myself and stayed out of his way as much as possible. But it was hard not to feel in the way when you're living in someone else's house and I began to miss my own place in Celbridge. I made an appointment to speak to someone in a women's support group about my situation and to find out what my rights were in relation to the house. The woman I met with advised me that if I wanted to retain any rights at all I would have to move back in and stake my claim.

So back I went.

Myself and Tyrone moved into the spare bedroom and tried to stay out of *Joseph*'s way as much as possible. It wasn't pleasant but we got by. Well, really, my best mate Mary helped me get by. Everyone needs someone to support them in times like that, and she was my someone.

I went into labour with my second baby a week early. Ma was with me when my waters broke and she rang a friend of *Joseph*'s who took me to the Rotunda Hospital in Dublin where I was shown to a waiting room full of other expectant mothers. Most of them had their partners with them. I envied them. *Joseph* hadn't been around for any of the check-ups or the antenatal classes, because we had agreed to separate. I loved being pregnant but I think it was probably the loneliest time in my life.

The fluid was still gushing out of me while I was seated in the waiting room. A small puddle had formed at my feet that was quickly becoming a lake. It was mortifying—I felt like I'd just gone to the loo in front of everybody. While the mothers-to-be all broke into a chorus of, 'Ahhh look, her waters just broke. She's going to have her baby,' the blokes beside them grew pale and looked like they were having second thoughts about holding their partners' hands during the birth.

For the second time, *Joseph* came back into my life for the birth of our child. I was annoyed at him for showing up. It felt like a charade but he was trying to make the best of a bad situation. Several hours of labour later, I had a beautiful baby girl who I named Robin. *Joseph* held her for a few minutes and oooh'ed and aaah'ed. At the time, I hated him for having come to the hospital at all but, looking back, I guess I'm glad he was there. Nowadays, my two kids love poring over old photographs and their eyes light up when they see the ones from the hospital with their da in them. It means a lot to them that their daddy loved them enough to see them being born.

Joseph eventually moved out of the house in Celbridge and moved to England. This time we split for good. So it was just me and my two babies now. With only me left to pay the mortgage, and no real income to my name, it wasn't long before I fell behind with payments and the mortgage company started threatening to repossess the house. I was left with no other choice but to put my babies in a crèche and get a job. It nearly tore me in two to leave them with strangers. But it was either that or become homeless.

I was thousands of pounds in arrears at this stage so the new job barely made a dent in things, but I liked the job and they liked me. I wasn't used to compliments or at least I never accepted them, but here I was told that I was a breath of fresh air around the place, and how intelligent I was. I had been feeling so utterly low after the breakdown of my relationship, so the timing was utterly perfect from my point of view. Beautiful things were said and my work was appreciated, and I began to feel someway towards 'normal'. I worked hard and remained focused on my children, choosing to remain celibate and on my own for the foreseeable future.

At home when I was alone at night, the horrors would start again. I've been a fan of the band Aslan for many years, and in the evenings I would put on their music and attempt to drown my sorrows with some wine. One song in particular tore at my heart when I listened to it. The title was 'Crazy World', and when I would hear the lyrics 'how can I protect you in this crazy world' I would sob deeply. It meant so many things to me. I couldn't help thinking of my own children and how desperately I wanted to protect them. I also cried because that's what my da should have been doing; it was his job to protect me. I'm proud to say that my children know I would do anything to keep them safe. It was when I was at home crying to this song that I realised I wasn't really keeping them safe as long as Da was still out on the streets. There was only one thing to do. As I sat listening to this anthem about protecting the ones you love, I knew I had to press charges against Da. It took me a little more time to build up the strength.

*

One day Ma rang me out of the blue to tell me that Da had been admitted to hospital 'cause of problems with his heart. I hadn't seen Da in years but I remember thinking to myself that I'd be in hospital too with a heart problem if I had the same things on my conscience as Da. I wouldn't be able to live with myself. It even crossed my mind that I didn't care if he died. But the second that thought occurred to me, I realised it wasn't true. I did care. Not because I felt sorry for him either or 'cause I wanted to make my peace with him. He was the one who had broken the peace. No, I didn't want him to die because I wanted justice. I wanted acknowledgement. I wanted to make sure that he never hurt another child again. I didn't want him to have a funeral with people crying over him. I knew exactly what the mourners would be saying:

'The poor man. And did you hear his horrible daughter stopped talking to him long before he died? Sure she didn't even come to his funeral.'

I wanted justice not just for me but for anyone else Da had hurt in the past. I guessed I wasn't the only one. They deserved to know that none of it was their fault. I felt that because I was his daughter it was more my responsibility than anyone else's to make right this wrong. And I wanted my children to be safe from people like my da in the future and for them to be proud of me for standing up to him.

I couldn't bear the thought of Da living in an estate full of small children and no one knowing how dangerous he was. I'd had enough.

After years and years of building up the courage, brick by brick, I finally decided to go to the gardaí.

When I made the decision to report Da, the gardaí began an investigation which located other women he had abused over the years. I managed to get in touch with these women and realised we were all on the same page and our objective was to press charges against my da, and name and shame him. It wasn't going to be easy and I was full of nerves but at least now I wasn't alone. The only thing that did isolate me from these girls was the fact that it was my da behind it all so while my family was affected they still had theirs to support them. We were all equally terrified though: terrified both for ourselves, and for the people around us, that a court case would have negative ripple effects on their lives.

Each meeting we had, I came away more and more shocked by what was revealed by the other girls. We started as a group of five but before long there were seven of us, all willing to prosecute. There were plenty more girls that we either heard of or spoke to directly who my da had abused too but, emotionally, they just weren't ready to go to the gardaí.

The courage and bravery of these women still astounds me and I'll never be able to thank them enough. For the first time in my life, I was surrounded by people who understood what I had been through; the shame and the guilt that had been weighing down on me since I was six years old. I've been asked countless times why I feel guilty and ashamed when I was just an innocent child and Da was clearly the one in the wrong. But unless you've been in the situation, then you can't possibly understand. And even if you have been there then, like me, you probably still won't fully understand it and will spend all your life trying to come to terms with it in your head.

Chapter Twelve

When I told my brothers that I was going to the guards, *Mark* offered to speak to them first, as a sort of icebreaker. He spoke to Detective Peter Cooney in Blanchardstown Garda Station and it was arranged that two female gardaí would talk to me. Before I knew what had hit me, I made a statement. The ball was rolling and there was nothing to do now but follow it all the way to its final resting point.

As a teenager, I hated the gardaí. They were the enemy—out to spoil our fun. Then again most figures of authority are a teenager's mortal enemy. But I found the gardaí from Blanchardstown fantastic to deal with all these years later. They handled my situation very delicately, even calling to my house to take my statements because they knew I'd be more comfortable there. I really felt like I could talk to the two female gardaí. It was like I had their trust from the very start. They were on my side. I spent hours and hours talking to them and telling them the gruesome details of the abuse that I'd never spoken aloud to anyone else before—

not even my counsellor. The words didn't come out easily; every single one was a struggle. For example, I'd refer to 'down there', and one of the gardaí would interrupt and ask, 'Is that your vagina you're referring to?' I'd just nod in reply. But the more I got to know these women, the more comfortable I felt revealing these details to them.

The statements went on for months until eventually, after I'd dissected every last memory from my childhood, the gardaí gave me back my finished statement to read over and make sure it was correct. Reading my statement was like reading about someone else's life. Had these things really happened to me? I felt sorry for the little girl in the statement. I wanted to gather her up in my arms and take her home with me so that I could mind her. I think that was when it hit me—the little girl in the statement was me. My da hadn't hurt Audrey Jude the adult, he had hurt Audrey Jude the child. And nobody was going to take Audrey the adult home and protect her. So I decided that I was going to have to start taking care of myself.

I thought once the statements had been given that Da would be arrested almost straight away and the court case would get underway. But it wasn't that straightforward. The statements were just the beginning of a process that would take several years.

Countless files were sent to the Director of Public Prosecutions and after each file a whole series of new questions arose and new evidence was unearthed. It was never-ending. But I had faith that in the end we'd get justice. I even found myself praying that nothing would happen to my da in the meantime. It would just leave me and all the other girls hanging in mid-air; my sanity depended on getting justice and acknowledgement for what had happened to us.

So I waited and waited.

I contacted Detective Cooney as regularly as I could. He was in charge of dealing with the mountain of paperwork and all the interviews for our case. In the beginning, I wouldn't talk to him about the case at all as he was a man and the details were just too intimate. But as time passed I started to trust him a great deal. He kept me informed on any development in the case—however small. But there could be months at a time when I wouldn't hear from him and I'd be climbing the walls in frustration. I just wanted—needed—to know that something was happening. But it was such a slow process. Detective Cooney was as frustrated as I was that it was taking so long. Like me, no garda officer likes to think of a child abuser living in a housing estate where none of the neighbouring families have any idea of the threat they pose. During this time, he moved to Cabra Garda Station (which happened to be the only other police station I'd gotten in trouble with when I was a teenager) but he continued to be my investigating officer and lifeline on the case.

While I was waiting for the case to come to court, I had plenty of other things on my plate to keep me occupied. Since the age of three, my son Tyrone had been behaving a little oddly, blinking his eyes uncontrollably and slapping himself every so often. He had also developed obsessive ritualistic behaviour. If the colour yellow wasn't featured somewhere on his clothes, he would refuse to leave the house. I'd have to get a yellow marker and draw a little dot on one of his socks to calm him down. Once we left the house, every few steps he took, he would jump into the air. When he spoke, he made occasional barking sounds or broke into high-pitched screeches. So I took him to doctor after doctor to try and find out what was wrong with him. Eventually a child psychiatrist diagnosed him with Tourettes Syndrome, accompanied by Obsessive Compulsive Behaviour. Attention Deficit Disorder was also later added to his diagnosis. Tyrone was never bold or hyperactive; he just had a short attention span.

I'd never heard of Tourettes Syndrome so when he was first diagnosed I was convinced that it was all my fault and that I had somehow transferred all my problems on to my poor baby. But I read up on the condition and found out that it's a gene defect that is mainly carried by males.

Tourettes Syndrome has gotten a fair bit of coverage in the media but the focus seems to be mainly on sufferers who blurt out bad language. This happens only with a small percentage of people. Although Tyrone blurts out words uncontrollably, they are never vulgar. Every so often he will have a good few weeks where the syndrome doesn't affect him too badly but then the next few weeks can be a nightmare. He seems to get worse at night-time. His body twitches a lot and keeps him awake. I have spent nights lying beside him, pinning his body down, while he cries out.

'Mammy, hold my body down. I'm so tired but it won't stop.'

My heart goes out to him.

I've found that the best way of dealing with it is to just do the best I can and even have a sense of humour about it if possible. I remember one time we were in a playground and Tyrone was walking about the place, with about eight little ones in a line behind him, copying his every move. He would take a few steps forward, stop, slap his thighs and jump in the air, genuflect and then start the pattern from scratch. The kids thought this was great fun. I find it's adults who lack patience and understanding.

So in the lead-up to the case I had my babies to mind and my finances to straighten out. I was so broke that I decided to speak to the Money Advice Bureau. They couldn't give me any financial assistance but they did talk to my bank and my mortgage company for me. They also contacted the Society of St Vincent de Paul and arranged for someone to come out and have a chat with me. They were very friendly but it still felt like an interview and I found the whole experience humiliating. I could remember donating tins of food to the St Vincent de Paul collections in the past and now here I was at the receiving end. As embarrassed as I was though, I was still extremely grateful. They gave me food vouchers for Tesco that I could use once a week, and at Christmas they gave me money to buy toys for the kids as well as a big hamper of food. They never made me feel like I was begging but rather that this was just a rough patch and that they were my training wheels until I could support myself again.

In part to help my finances, I sold the house in Celbridge and moved to Virginia in County Cavan with my two children. I found a lovely three-bedroom house.

The garden was smaller than Celbridge, but the rest of the house was just as big so I didn't feel like I had down-graded. In fact, for the first time ever I had three toilets, which was a novelty.

I picked this town because it was affordable, plus it seemed lovely with a lake, and the school was only at the top of our estate. I didn't know anyone there so it was a huge move for me and the two kids on our own. But financially I had no choice and we needed a fresh start. We moved in September just in time for the kids to start school. My daughter Robin was starting in junior infants and my son Tyrone in second class.

I brought the kids to school and was left on my own for a couple of hours every day. I had already registered myself with the doctors in Virginia, mortified with the big bulky records they would be receiving from my old doctor. But the new doctor was very nice and continued to help me and I got the prescriptions I needed to survive.

I suddenly had a lot of time to think and I realised I had not seen pictures of me as a child during my adulthood. This struck me and opened a curiosity and yearning in me. I found the courage and wrote to my Ma asking her for pictures of me from my childhood. I hadn't spoken to her in years but I was delighted when she wrote back and sent me some photos.

The pictures showed me as a little girl, and brought back lots of memories, unsettling memories. In the picture, I could see this little girl looking back at me and I knew her. It was me; behind the smile I was hurt, in pain and innocent. It was a very emotional moment and I was glad I was on my own. I cried bitterly for the little girl in the photo. She had done nothing to deserve what had happened to her. It made me more determined to get justice for this little girl. Up until this point, I had only ever seen myself as an adult, and I could only see Da abusing me as an adult. When I looked in the mirror, it was the adult that I saw. This was not the person he abused. It was a little innocent child who was lost inside me, somewhere hiding. She was looking out through adult eyes from inside my brain. But she was still there; I could feel her and her pain. I could hear her calling out to me for help. She needed me to carry on and I was going to do my best to save her. Now that I was an adult I could do that for her and no one was going to get in my way. She needed peace; to lie down and have a long deserved sleep, safely and loved in my memories. She was so tired.

*

In the midst of all this drama, the only thing keeping me sane was my social nights out. I was back socialising and, yes, I was back using drugs every now and again. I hadn't taken any during either pregnancy or when the kids were small and I never brought any into the house. But it was something that I needed to do for myself every so often just to take the edge off things. So my nights out consisted of a few drinks and a few lines of coke. Cocaine made me feel alive again. It was like having adrenalin injected into sleepy joints. It also kept me happy. If I'd been relying on the drink alone, I'd probably have spent most nights stooped over my pint, tears running down my cheeks and into the glass. Cocaine was expensive but luckily I never had to buy it myself. It was usually passed around if you were sitting in a group. I didn't see myself as having a problem. It was purely a social thing and if it helped me to function then I reasoned that it was medicinal.

*

My emotional state was fragile so when Detective Cooney finally rang me and told me he'd arrested Da and taken him in for questioning at around 7am that morning, I thought I might tip over the edge.

Da initially confessed to being an abuser in the interview room, but then got annoyed.

'I'm disgusted that you're making such a fuss over something that happened so long ago. It's ridiculous that you're putting me through this,' he is said to have complained.

He still couldn't see how terrible his crime was. He showed absolutely no remorse. He was more concerned about how this would affect his life. So much for the counselling he got. Wasn't it supposed to make him understand the effects his abuse had had on people?

I knew things would probably get worse before they got better but at that time I felt like I was close to rock bottom. I was taking antidepressants and sleeping tablets just to stay afloat. The sleeping tablets were a better substitute for alcohol in helping me get to sleep but before long I was completely addicted to them. If I tried to go a night without them, I wouldn't get a wink of sleep.

Going to the gardaí had been like opening Pandora's Box 'cause my nightmares had become more frequent and vivid. It was like every last demon from my past had been unleashed. The nightmares were different to the ones in the past but the exact same fear lay at the root of them all. I would find myself outside my house looking in my front window where I'd see Da sitting with Robin perched on his knees. He'd be smirking at me. I'd open my mouth to scream as loud as I could but nothing would come out. I'd try banging on the window but no one could hear me. Da had my daughter and I was helpless. In another nightmare, I was at some sort of a children's day out and I could see my da in the distance holding hands with two little girls as they skipped away from the rest of the people. I went running up to the parents to warn them about my da but no one would believe me. I screamed at them but they would just brush me away like a fly.

It got to the stage where I was scared to go to sleep at night. Scared of re-entering a world where Da had all the power. My body would fight against the clock, refusing to surrender. In the end, the tablets were the only way of knocking myself out and getting a few hours sleep. But I often wondered if it was worth it. I always woke up more tired than I'd been before going to sleep; probably because I'd spent the whole night tossing and turning and trying to outrun my da.

To cope with the sleepless nights and subsequent horrific nightmares, not to mention my son's sleeping problems, I went back to the doctor and got stronger sleeping pills, as well as maximum strength anxiety tablets, which I took alongside the sleeping tablets at night. I just wanted to conk out and stop my brain from hurting at night. My doctor was very supportive and could see I was on the edge. She arranged for me to see a psychiatrist, who gave me a few sessions, increased my antidepressants and referred me to a psychologist.

These sessions were a real boost for me. The psychologist did IQ tests and I scored very high, in the top percentage. Any little sign of nice feedback was always welcome to me. It also made me sad, though, that I didn't study and go to college. I obviously had the capability.

He did various other tests and told me I was pretty sane except for the problems I had suffered as a child. At this point I had not associated any of my phobias or emotional distresses with my past. This was just the beginning of my coming to terms with the effect the abuse had on me.

Chapter Thirteen

Eventually I accepted that I needed professional counselling to work through my nightmares, and to give me the strength to deal with pressing charges against Da. The psychologist referred me to the Rian group in Cavan and I found that I enjoyed going there. My counsellor talked to me in a different way than others and had a great way of looking at things from a new angle.

I was still addicted to sleeping tablets, antidepressants and anti-anxiety tablets but I was feeling full of hope and brighter. I had, like anyone, both ups and downs.

Seeing this counsellor was a turning point in my life. She concentrated on the positive things I had achieved, and helped me see for the first time how much I had done on my own. This made me feel good. She explained to me how my phobias and rituals were coping skills and survival skills. I had nothing to be ashamed of. She gave me strength and slowly but surely I began to see myself as a different person: a good person; a gentle person.

Although I was still taking cocaine, it was not on a regular basis—less than once a month. I kept this away from the house and children and never took it around people who didn't use it. I never introduced it to anyone 'cause I knew it was a fool's way of having a good time. These are not excuses; I am just telling you how it was.

But my tiredness was getting worse. I hadn't felt well for a while and my back was very sore. I put everything down to stress until one day a friend suspected something was wrong with me and called to my house. When there was no answer, she let herself in and found me almost convulsing, with a dangerously high temperature. The bed was soaking with sweat.

It turned out that I had serious kidney problems, and I needed an operation. I spent several weeks in hospital and got out just before Christmas. It was a terrible time and I was so lonely for my children. Because I couldn't be with them, I started developing terrible fears that something might happen to them, and that Da might try to contact them. My friends were taking care of the children while I was ill, however, and they knew the situation and understood how I felt. They reassured me that no one would get near them without my authorisation, and once I knew they were safe I was able to concentrate on getting better.

As I lay waiting on the operation table, it suddenly struck me: 'I am really sick.' This was no spoof, and I wasn't pretending. I genuinely deserved to be there and get the nursing I needed. It was a good feeling; that I wasn't lying or deceiving. I didn't have to make up pains and try to convince them. They could see from my test results and x-rays what was wrong with me. It was a weird feeling after being in and out of hospital as a child, to actually be really sick.

I couldn't drive till March that year with the pain, but as soon as I could I got straight back into counselling. I had become more withdrawn during my illness and was quite self-absorbed. So much was happening with my health and finances and I was constantly waiting to hear when the court case would be.

I was riddled with guilt and anguish over Da. I worried about whether he had access to children. I expressed this opinion to the social workers over and over. Nothing else mattered; no one else mattered. Other people could do what they wanted in their lives. I had this heavy load to carry and couldn't see past it.

*

Out of the blue I received a phone call on my mobile; it was Detective Cooney telling me they were officially arresting my da the following day for the purpose of charging him. I was a bundle of nerves that night and my stomach was sick. I imagined how it would be done in my head, between S.W.A.T. teams and all sorts. Of course it wasn't as dramatic as all that. I felt sorry for my ma, wondering if she was going to be there when the police arrived. I told no one in case it didn't happen.

The first thing on my mind was to ring my best friend in England; the second thing was to remember to breathe. Despite waiting all these years, I was in shock. My body and brain didn't know how to react. I spent that night and the following days talking non-stop to people who knew the story.

Within weeks Da had to appear at a number of court dates to hear the charges. There were dozens of sample charges that had to be formally dealt with. I didn't go to any of these court hearings; I didn't have the nerve. I just waited for Detective Cooney to ring me after each one and fill me in on what was happening.

I couldn't help but wonder how Da was coping with this. Did he go home after being read the charges of child abuse and have his tea? I found it all very weird. Did he go to the Blanchardstown shopping centre or into Arnotts and have lunch, as he usually did on Saturdays? I couldn't fathom how he lived or what planet he was living on. Luckily I had the Rian group to talk to and to help me through this.

The counselling sessions made me stronger, more determined to expose my father and reveal him as a paedophile. I was sick of hiding.

I continued reading and researching inner peace, looking for a way to rid myself of any anger or injustices I had in my life. I finally found 'independence' in 2007.

By this I mean I now felt completely mentally independent. I realised I had always relied on what other people thought of me to make me happy or to make a decision.

From the summer 2007 I started to like myself and have faith in what I did. As a consequence of this I became happier. I cut out any negative thinking and stopped listening to negative people. I was getting strong again and preparing for what I would have to face.

My faith in God was growing and I continued to pray even when the going got tough. I believe in Karma and know that if you live a good life, then good things happen. If you cannot do something good for anyone the best thing you can do is to make a conscious decision to do no harm.

As the court case drew closer, I realised with surprise that I knew I would be able to face whatever came my way. The worst part was all behind me. My father could no longer hurt me. I hoped he would no longer be able to hurt anyone in the future.

Out of the blue I got a phone call to say that the court date was set. It was time to face my da again after all these years.

Chapter Fourteen

I spent most of the night before the court hearing on the phone to my friend Mary. I thought if I just kept talking, and barely even stopped to take a breath, then I might be able to keep my fears at bay. I was on the phone to Mary for about three hours. She was living in London and couldn't make the trial the next day but she was flying home the following day to be with me.

'You're strong,' she kept reassuring me. 'You've been through worse than this so I know you can get through it.'

She told me that what I wore on the day could be very important. I told her I had two potential suits—a red one and a cream one.

'Don't wear the red one to court,' she said immediately.

I didn't know what all the fuss was about but I decided it was better to be safe than sorry so I went with the cream one.

I made arrangements for the kids to be minded by my friend Michelle's au pair throughout the trial. So the following morning, Michelle drove with me to Dublin. She tried to keep my mind off things on the way by chatting about anything but the trial. At one stage we were passing a group of people picketing to 'Save Tara'—the Hill of Tara heritage site in County Meath that was under threat of being destroyed to make way for a new motorway. Michelle tried to distract me by flying into a big one-sided debate about the Tara supporters and her views on the whole thing. Normally, I'd be up for a good debate but today I just looked at her and said, 'Michelle I'm on my way to court today to testify against me da for sexually abusing me. I'm sorry if I'm not feeling especially passionate about Tara right now.'

There was nothing to do but laugh at the situation.

'You're right, it doesn't seem as important this morning, does it?' said Michelle.

I insisted on driving to Dublin 'cause I needed to focus my mind on something other than the case. We stopped for petrol along the way and the attendant gave us both the once-over with a cheeky look in his eyes.

'You look lovely girls. Going somewhere nice?' he asked.

'Yeah,' was all I could bring myself to say.

In fairness, I'd say he would have preferred this short answer to the long one. We'd have been there all day.

When we arrived at Cabra Garda Station, we parked the car and met with Detective Cooney and one of his colleagues. Myself and Michelle piled into the back of the Garda car and they drove us to the pub The Legal Eagle, which was near the Four Courts. I was meeting the other six girls there who had pressed charges against Da.

Before we got out of the car, Detective Cooney turned around and handed me a letter.

'It's from your father,' he said.

This was the first contact I'd had from Da in years. My hands were shaking as I opened the letter. It read:

Castleknock
Dublin 15
21 January 2008

Dear Audrey,

I know that when I offered to apologise some time ago, through Mam, you said that you were not quite ready and that you would prefer to make the first move when you were.

However, things are very different now, and I wish to offer my most sincere, abject and humble apologies for all the hurt and upset I caused you.

I cannot understand my behaviour, although I am working hard with some very good people who are helping me a lot, and making good progress.

It is terrible that we should come to this, after all the fun we had camping and boating, and the gym and toning centre, where we thought we were going to make our fortunes. But it was not to be.

I was the cause of spoiling that great relationship.

I hope you will find it in your heart to accept my deeply felt and sincerely meant apologies for every hurt and pain I caused you ever.

Love, Dad

I couldn't believe what I'd read. As far as I was concerned, Da had learned nothing from the counselling if he thought that I had enjoyed all those holidays. Did he think it was possible to separate what had happened during the night from what had happened during the day? Did he not realise that he had polluted everything? How could I accept his apology when he didn't even understand what he was apologising for?

He must have known all those years ago that what he was doing to me would have lasting effects. If nothing else, he knew it was illegal. But he chose to satisfy his own fetish and continue doing it—not just to me but to other little girls as well. A few years ago his letter would have torn me in two. Today, it was just confirmation that he hadn't changed.

When we got to the pub, a group of us gathered around a table. Some fabulous relatives of mine, including my godmother and an uncle, turned up to support me. The other six women also had friends and relatives there too. Introductions were made but after that hardly anything was said. Cups of coffee were passed around though most people were secretly itching for something stronger to calm their nerves. The tension in the pub was terrible but we all knew that we hadn't long to go now.

I had decided some time before the trial to waive my right to anonymity. I was the only one of the seven of us prosecuting my da to do so. But I felt that the public needed a face that they could identify with. So before we headed into the Four Courts, I agreed to pose for photographs for the media. I knew they needed the pictures in order to get the story out and that had been one of the main motivations behind this court case after all. From the beginning it had been a mutual agreement: name and shame him. So I stood outside the courthouse, across from the River Liffey, with the strong wind playing havoc with my hair, while what seemed like a billion and one camera lenses were aimed in my direction. It was freezing and the photos took longer than I'd expected. The thought of Da driving by while I was there terrified me. I didn't like the idea of him being able to see me when I couldn't see him. It brought me back to the old skin-crawling, stomach-churning feeling of my teenage years when his eyes followed me everywhere.

When the photos were finally over, I raced back into the pub for a hot cuppa. It wasn't long before Detective Cooney phoned and told us it was time for us to go over to the courthouse. My legs were shaking so badly I wasn't sure if I'd be able to walk across. My uncle ended up practically carrying me.

*

My father had offered to plead guilty to a number of sample charges which meant that we didn't have to undergo a cross examination against him. But I was still terrified at seeing him again after all the years.

My biggest fear was walking into the courtroom and not knowing where he was sitting. He'd see me before I'd see him. I had to take a breather at the door of the courthouse. I lent against a wall, rocking back and forth, willing myself not to throw up. It had taken me so many years to get here, yet I wasn't sure now whether or not I could actually go through with it. It needed to be done but I just wished somebody else could do it for me.

'I'm not going in till someone tells me where my da is,' I said to my uncle. 'Is he even in there yet?'

He ran off to check. When he came back he told me, 'Your Ma and Da are already in there.'

My body was trembling. It wasn't fair that I had to do this. It took every ounce of energy I had left to pull myself away from the wall and walk into the courtroom. I took a seat at the very back of the room.

I could hear people whispering and sobbing in different corners of the room. I didn't realise my own sobs were part of the chorus.

The more I tried to stop myself from crying, the more my lips quivered and the more I found myself gasping for air. I was making a right racket but I couldn't control myself. Next thing I knew, my three brothers had filed in beside me, forming a human wall that protected me from my da's line of vision. I couldn't see him now but he couldn't see me either. I felt my breathing slowly return to normal.

As the case got underway, descriptions of the abuse that I was forced to endure were read into evidence. All I heard was, 'His daughter Audrey, something something, "vagina".'

Christ, the word had been said in front of everyone. My brothers, friends and relatives. All of a sudden, I knew I didn't want everyone listening to what had happened to me. I panicked, and although the power had gone out of my legs, it hadn't gone out of my lungs.

'Can everyone leave the court please?' I shouted. My fear of the court had disappeared.

A lot of people began to file out of the room, including most of my male relatives, but a lot of other people stayed and I wasn't happy about that. I knew they were sitting there to support their own friends or family but I hated them hearing the intimate and explicit details of my past. A friend of mine was sitting on my left hand side and I used her body to conceal my face because, with the courtroom half-empty, I felt exposed again. I asked her to stick her fingers in her ears when the worst details were being read out.

Every so often, I peeked out from behind my friend to look at my parents. I couldn't imagine what it was like for them, especially Ma, being in her position and listening to the same list of crimes against her own daughter.

A little while later, our barrister asked the judge for a short break and I made a dart for the door. I ran straight into the arms of my uncle and started bawling.

My friend Michelle took me by the arm and brought me to the loo where she washed the pools of mascara off my cheeks and helped me tidy up my face. My eyes were red and bulging and my vision was blurred.

Back in the hallway, my barrister came up to me.

'Will you take the stand?' she asked.

'Yes,' I croaked.

I knew I had to. This judge didn't know who I was but I hoped that if she heard me speak, my victim impact statement might seem more real to her. One of the other girls agreed to take the stand too and I was so proud of her.

Detective Cooney knew how terrified I was of having Da's eyes on me so he offered to block his view by walking me up to the stand and walking me back down afterwards. So, carrying a tissue and a bottle of water in one hand, and holding on to his arm for dear life with the other, I walked up to the box.

My barrister tried to ease me into the questions at first. I remember very little of what was said.

I described feeling isolated, mistrustful of men and overprotective of my own children. 'My father's guilty plea is the only thing I will say "thank you" for.'

I also remember repeating, 'My heart is just broken,' over and over as the barrister asked me questions about how the abuse had affected me.

'When your dad does that and your mam stands by him, it just makes you feel worthless,' I told the judge.

I read in one newspaper that Da bowed his head and wept for what he had done, as I said this, but I have no recollection of this.*

I was so conscious of Da's eyes on me that I couldn't bring myself to look in his direction. I didn't want to hurt Ma; I just wanted her to know that her little girl, her only baby girl, was hurting.

But I wasn't the only one. The others had described in their victim impact reports and statements how they suffered from suicidal feelings, mistrust of men, panic attacks and insomnia. It is important to remember that it wasn't just me who had suffered.

---

* Evidence given in the Dublin Circuit Criminal Court.

The barristers who represented my father pleaded for leniency to be shown and said he had also suffered.

Da was described as a retired man who was now 'a pariah in his own family' and who would be 'watched by a hawk's eye' when he was around children.

'He is punished every day in a very real way,' said a member of his defence team, who also said that Ma had found herself in 'an appalling dilemma'.

His defence team had also mentioned that Da had voluntarily attended counselling in the early 1990s and appreciated how traumatic the abuse had been.*

*

When Detective Cooney walked me back down from the stand I made straight for the exit. I could feel my heart racing and a lump had sprung up in my throat. No one could make me feel better. No one could make me feel any worse.

Judge Delahunt broke for lunch at 1p.m. and told us to come back at 2p.m. I was under the impression that the sentence would be announced then and that would be the end of it.

Leaving the courtroom, I headed straight to the bathroom and who did I run into only Ma and Da. As soon as I spotted them, I spun on my heels and ran in the opposite direction. It was like a reflex reaction. My mates and family said they never saw anyone in high heels sprint

---

* Evidence given in the Dublin Circuit Criminal Court.

so fast across the courtyard and around the corner. I was like the roadrunner being fuelled by pure panic. I didn't stop running till I got to The Legal Eagle. When the rest of them caught up with me, they couldn't stop laughing over the speed of me despite my three-inch heels. The teasing helped lighten the mood.

During lunch, everyone kept telling me how brave I was.

'But did you not see me? I was shitting it. How can you say I was brave?' I asked.

'Your courage shone through. You did brilliant. I don't know how you did it at all,' was the reply.

I was a trembling wreck though. As far as I was concerned, 2p.m. couldn't come quick enough. I just wanted to get it over with. My friends were all trying to force food into me but hunger was the last thing on my mind.

'I'll just puke if I eat anything,' I said pushing the plates away from me.

We filed back into the courtroom at 2p.m. on the dot. When everyone was seated and silenced, the judge made a speech, most of which meant very little to me, before adjourning the case for two weeks.

Another two weeks of waiting. I didn't think I was able for it.

Back in the pub, I had a good think about it. Originally, I'd been angry that the details of the case weren't being given enough time and attention so really I was happy that the judge was delaying sentencing to do just this, although I knew I would be living on my nerves for the next two weeks.

A few gin and tonics later I headed home. I wasn't driving this time of course. I was dying to get back to my kids. I had kept them informed on the details of the case as much as I could considering their ages. Robin was only eight, while Tyrone was eleven.

'We're the good guys,' I had told them, 'And we're fighting against the bad guys who hurt children.'

Robin was a little confused at first. She thought that if Da didn't get put away then this meant I would go to jail but I set her straight immediately. I wanted to be as honest and open with them as possible.

Back at the house, I found one of the dogs had decided to use the kitchen floor as his toilet so I got to work cleaning the mess up. Between that and getting the kids ready for bed, I wasn't long settling back into reality.

*

The following day, my best friend Mary flew over from England and she took me out for a few drinks. It was lovely having her there. Mary is the kind of friend who never judges or criticises you. Just because she may not necessarily understand something, doesn't mean she has to try and take over the situation and come up with a solution. She takes me as I am, warts and all. We balance each other out—she's the practical one and I'm the emotional one. Having her there the weekend after the hearing was brilliant. By the time she left, I felt calmer and more prepared for the next two weeks of clock-watching.

As the two weeks crept slowly by, I began to think about what outfit to wear to the sentencing. I only had two suits to my name; I'd already worn the cream one but everyone seemed dead set against me wearing the red one. I still couldn't understand why but I was in no frame of mind to be asking questions or making decisions that week. So I went and bought myself a nice black skirt and jacket.

The day before the sentencing, I had the dogs in the room with me as I was getting my outfit together. When I turned around, I saw one of the dogs making for the doorway with a familiar-looking black object clenched between his teeth. It was one of my shoes. I ran after him but by the time I'd wrestled the shoe back he had it half-chewed to bits. I was devastated. I spent the next hour ringing around trying to find someone with a size-three foot who could give me a loan. It all seemed so important at the time. Like what I wore could really change the judge's mind. But it was easier to focus on small stuff like this, than let my mind wander on to the bigger stuff.

*

On the day of the sentencing, we all gathered in the courtroom early. I had Mary on one side of me holding my hand and another good friend on the other side. We'd already spent the last two weeks waiting.

I really didn't know what to expect. Judge Delahunt explained that changes in legislation during the period in which Da had abused me and the others meant the maximum penalty available to her in some of the cases was two years' imprisonment, while the sentence available in the later offences was ten years. She said it was important that we understood this so we didn't think she was minimising the impact of the abuse.

Then she began to deliver the sentence. It was a surreal moment. She said she took into account the multiplicity of the charges, the number and young ages of the victims, and the fact that his actions represented a breach of trust and that he abused some of his victims while other people were present.

Then she began listing all the different charges and for each one she read out a jail sentence. They were only sample charges but they added up to 32 years in total. At the end of all this, the judge announced, 'Bernard Delaney is to be given a sentence of five years, of which four are to be served in custody and one year suspended. He is also to continue treatment.'

So what had happened to the other 27 years? How did 32 suddenly become 5? My head was spinning.

Then I thought, Christ, Da is going to prison. It was so hard to take in. He was a professional man, with designer suits and all. After all this time you would think I would be prepared. But I never wanted to visualise this day, as it hurt too much. It was definitely the outcome I knew I wanted—justice, acknowledgement.

I would have been devastated if he had gotten off, or received a suspended sentence, so I was pleased with the custodial sentence. To me, it meant the justice system takes it seriously when a man hurts and sexually abuses a child. He was now on the sex offenders register; it was all confusing and my heart was racing. I left the courtroom as soon as it was over and ran towards the glass so I could stare out and shed some more tears without having to see Da leave. Plus it gave me a private window in my head to make sense of it.

I just stared out the window, trembling, as people poured through the court doors. All I wanted was a drink. The reporters took a step back, giving me time to take in what had happened. I knew they wanted their story and I had chosen to waive my right to anonymity. There was no point in doing all this in my eyes without using it to give strength to others. The atmosphere was chaotic.

'What happened, what did he get?'

Everyone was confused, especially me. This had been the end to a long emotionally pulled battle between my mind, heart, body and soul.

The only thing that really mattered though was that we had won. The law had sided with us and had recognised all the damage and wrong Da had done. So many cases likes ours never even make it past the DPP due to lack of evidence or proof. Either that or the poor victim drops the charges because they're not mentally able for the trial.

I knew that we had accomplished something great by overcoming all the obstacles. The judge and the guards had trusted us and believed in us. And I felt that maybe just maybe I could start to do the same.

Afterwards, outside the courthouse, people were keen to fill me in on his reaction.

'Your da looked shocked—in complete disbelief.'

'You could see the fear in his eyes as they were handcuffing him.'

*

How did I feel about the outcome? I certainly wasn't outraged. I knew I could never get complete justice for what had happened. I was completely split in two. The fight was over and he was locked up. I knew he was shocked and hurt. I felt sorry for him when the judge handed out the sentence. He looked amazed, stunned and was in a state of utter disbelief. I had to turn away. I didn't want him to see me. I guess it's normal to still have some sort of bond with a parent. But I couldn't let that get in the way of what he did. Here I was feeling sorry for him and I was broken-hearted myself. It went against the grain to take your own da to court.

The strongest feeling overriding all the emotions mixed up inside me was I DID IT. We did it. Me—this little person who had only two weeks ago sat four feet away from Da, violently shaking while answering questions. I collapsed a few times and my legs went like jelly.

I was not a bit disappointed with the result. I feel these guys should be locked up forever, but that's not going to happen. So instead he has to sit there night after night, week after week knowing he has four years to serve.

I on the other hand was aware he would be out in four years. I wanted it to be known what he was capable of, so that when he does get out, people would be aware of what he had done. Children should be protected. He was being named and shamed.

Da was taken away in a prison van. He was heading to jail for one of the worst crimes there is. Da had been locked up for being a paedophile. Surely, there was no more room for denial.

I'm sure Da was probably still wondering what all the fuss was about. How had it come to this? Sure, he hadn't done very much had he? It had all happened so long ago. Everyone was making a big deal out of nothing and blowing it out of all proportion. I wondered if he was scared as he was led out of the courtroom. Was he worried about what lay ahead of him—of the hard men that he was going to be thrown in with? I couldn't bear to think of him in his cell. I know others wanted him to suffer but that wasn't how I felt. All I'd wanted all along was for Da to realise what he was doing and stop. I just wanted the abuse to stop somewhere.

So while Da was being led to his new home for the next four years, I headed straight for the pub. There were loads of us gathered there but I think me and the six other girls felt very much separate to everyone else—like we were members of a secret club. Friends and relatives were offering us all sorts of advice on how to move on with our lives. But a lot of the well-meant advice was not what I wanted or needed. I think every one of us just wanted to feel like we were back in control of our lives after lifetimes of doubt and worry.

It wasn't long before the media were hot on my heels looking for their interviews. I was the only one of the seven victims to waive my right to anonymity so all the pressure to get our message out to the general public fell on my shoulders. With the others by my side, I went back over to the Four Courts to face the cameras. I couldn't believe the number of photographers and reporters awaiting me. But, surprisingly, I didn't feel scared. Something was driving me on; somewhere deep inside me there was a voice screaming for release.

Standing before all the media, I read the statement that had been in my head for years. I started off by thanking the people who had helped put my da behind bars; the six other girls, as well as the dedication of Detective Cooney. I said what it meant to us.

This is by no means closure for any of us or for the other poor sufferers this man has preyed on. He took a sense of innocence and self-worth away from all of us and left us with a pain in our hearts that will never be healed. The issues we carried yesterday, we still have to deal with tomorrow and the next day. On a daily basis, our families feel the hurt and the knock-on effect of what he has done.

Putting my father, Bernard Delaney, in prison was not an act of revenge as it doesn't really make a difference to us seven women whether or not he is locked up; he has already done his utmost damage to us. But it will make a difference to you the public, to your children, your nieces and nephews, brothers, sisters and grandchildren. We have managed to take one paedophile off the streets in an effort to save future innocent little spirits.

I went on to say what was most important to me about this case.

I would like to appeal to the general public to do the same. If you know of a paedophile, please stand up and pass the shame on to them. It isn't your shame to suffer with. Give the abused—whether they are still young or have reached adulthood—the support and backing they will need to expose these violators. It is a horrific crime. I am doing my best to protect your children, please do the same for mine. This crime is all too often swept under the carpet in this country for various reasons but at the end of the day the safety and well-being of our children is all that matters. It shouldn't matter if in-laws, neighbours or anyone else is afraid of the effect coming clean may have on them. All you need is one person who is on your side and willing to help you.

Somebody had to be prepared to put themselves on the line for these innocent and defenceless kids. I am sorry that it took so long to get our case to court. It took years and years and during that time we were not allowed to speak publicly about our abuser or we would never have got him off the streets today. I have chosen to go public in the hope that I might be able to give hope and strength to others. But our legal system allows you to remain anonymous if you so wish.

As a mother, I would not have been able to call myself a good person knowing there was a paedophile living in Dublin with access to your children. I would hope others feel the same and that they would be willing to protect my children if the time came. These violations are not one-off crimes, they are compulsions that will make the abuser offend again and again until somebody stops them.

This case was never about causing anarchy as this is of no benefit to the sufferers in the long run. It was about giving broken children or adults everywhere acknowledgement and vindication and, above all, giving them a second chance in life. My aim is to educate children on what abuse is; how it starts, how manipulators can groom you over a period of time and how the person closest to you can often be the one you should most fear. It's not just the infamous stranger in the car with sweets that children should stay clear of. Most abusers are known and loved by their victims. That is why it is so difficult to speak up.

Seven of us came forward in this case but we are representing many others whom we know have been affected by this man. We hope that this outcome will not only help us to put the past behind us but that it might also safeguard the future of our precious little children.

*

Back at the pub, the drink continued to flow. But my emotions were running so high that I needed something more; something to keep the dark thoughts away. So I secretly got some cocaine and sniffed it for what I swore would be the last time. I didn't really consider coke a problem—I was more addicted to the anxiety tablets and the sleeping pills. But that night, even though we had gotten the verdict we wanted, I didn't feel happy and I needed something to stop the downward spiral. I couldn't stop thinking about Da. At one point in the evening I turned around to one of my friends and said, 'Jesus, my da is spending his first night in the cell, it's unbearable to think about it.'

'Don't think about it,' my friend advised. 'Just try to go back and get some sleep.'

Myself and Mary had booked into a bed and breakfast in Malahide on the outskirts of Dublin for the next two nights. I was in no state to drive all the way home and I needed to take a little time out before returning to the real world.

I went back to the B&B and took my sleeping pills and tranquillisers. The couple who owned the B&B couldn't have been nicer to me. They treated me like a princess. I had a lovely long lie-in, a killer breakfast and one of the staff even went to the shop and brought back that day's papers for me. I couldn't believe it when I saw my face sprawled across nearly every front page.

Some of the papers published a nice write-up and had gotten in all of the main points of my statement, but I was so disappointed to see that others reduced it to a mere tabloid headline. Printed above a picture of me in one tabloid was the headline 'My Sex Beast Dad' in huge bold print. They had basically printed the opposite to my message. I wanted the public to understand that it's not 'beasts' who abuse children but statistically it is more often loved ones who abuse. They are not strange-looking creatures that have horns and jump out from behind trees. They do not look like beasts, which means that it's much harder for a child to identify these people as dangerous.

Tyrone and Robin were staying with a friend of mine and I had warned her not to bring them into any newsagents for sweets as my face was everywhere—rows and rows of me pictured from different angles.

That night, after a lot of hesitation, myself and Mary decided to go out for a few drinks in Malahide. Heads started turning the second we walked into the pub. People were reading the day's newspapers, with my face splashed across them, and they now kept looking from their newspaper to me, and back again, trying to figure out if it was definitely me. One woman spent the entire night staring at me, her head twisted at what looked like a very awkward angle. Myself and Mary just laughed at her. Many people put their newspapers aside to come up and give me a hug and tell me how brave they thought I was. I was happy people came over and spoke to me—it was much better than just being stared at. At least then I that knew they were on my side and thought I had done the right thing.

One lady decided to start a singsong later on in the night but her choice of song wasn't the most appropriate. She chose 'Tie a Yellow Ribbon Round the Old Oak Tree', which is a song about someone in prison. She didn't even realise what she was singing about until she was halfway through the song. She was going to stop but I was laughing so hard I nearly fell off the chair. Even in my mixed state of grief and triumph, I was still able to appreciate the irony of the song.

The following day, I'd had my fill of the royal treatment and was dying to see my kids again. I dropped Mary to Dublin Airport for her flight home and went straight to my friend's to pick up the kids. We passed by Mountjoy Prison on the way home and I pointed it out to Robin and Tyrone.

'Now kids,' I said, 'We are passing by a big prison where people who have broken the law are put. See that big grey building? Isn't it huge?'

I never called my father their granddad because in my eyes he hadn't earned that privilege, so Robin and Tyrone always called him 'Mammy's da'.

'God Ma, it is huge. There must be an awful lot of bad people in the world,' said Robin.

'There are but once they're sent there you're safe from them. Even if my father ever was to escape, he still wouldn't be able to hurt anyone because Mammy made sure to get his name and face all over the news so that everyone will know what he looks like and be able to keep their babies safe like I do.'

'You're brilliant, Ma. You helped save a lot of children. Why doesn't everyone do that?'

'I can't speak for everyone, pet, but I want to help change that.'

'Cool, can I tell my mates?' Tyrone asked.

'You sure can, honey, and be proud,' I told him smiling at him.

Over the next few days, I showed Robin and Tyrone a few newspaper articles along with some choice lines on how brave I was and their little faces lit up with pride. I wanted to explain things to them 'cause I wanted to make sure that they heard it properly from me rather than a Chinese-Whispers version in the playground.

I went into a state of shock when we got back to Virginia. I couldn't leave the house for the first few days. I was so worn out that I felt like I could sleep for weeks. So I kept the kids close to me and waited till we ran out of food before braving the local EuroSpar. I was scared of how the locals would react to me after all the media coverage of the case. But I have to say, I never got a warmer welcome in my life. They couldn't have been nicer and it certainly took the sting out of re-entering the community.

Life didn't sit around waiting for me to be ready to deal with it after the court case. I just had to try and get on with things as best I could. My daughter's First Communion became my next big focus. It took place a few weeks after the case and I was glad of the distraction.

She had to receive her first confession a number of weeks before her communion. It was done by a wonderful priest who is very good with the children, Fr Dermott. I decided to get confession with her in support of her big night. God knows what Fr Dermott thought when I went up.

'Bless me Father for I have sinned. It is 25 years since my last confession. . .'

He didn't even flinch. 'Well, we will start from now,' he replied gently.

I didn't even get any penance. I expected to be on my knees for an hour doing 100 decades of the rosary. I felt good after confession. Not that I had felt bad before it. I just felt a little lighter and used it as a start for myself to be good.

The health board came to my rescue with money for a communion dress, and my godmother and one of my cousins threw a tremendous party for Robin in Dublin which she is still talking about several months later. Her daddy even made it to the church.

Chapter Fifteen

Having dealt with the most traumatic part of my life, I knew I would have the strength to deal with what I could not have done in the past. I realised that I could no longer attempt to fill the void inside me with medicine, drugs and drink and it was for this reason I decided to detox and take action to help me overcome my addiction to this crutch.

I figured it was time to lay my final ghost to rest, for my sake, and for the sake of my children. In the summer following the trial, I headed off for a three-week retreat to Thamkrabok Monastery Drug Treatment and Rehabilitation Centre in Thailand where I hoped to reconnect with the little girl inside me that I had lost contact with all those years ago.

I stepped off the plane in Bangkok, surprised that the 16-hour journey hadn't been as hard as I thought. Then again when you're pumped up on Valium and sleeping pills, everything seems okay.

The wonderful heat hit me as I stepped out of the airport, and I realised that I was in a different world. Thamkrabok Monastery sent someone to collect me, and after a two-hour drive, I arrived at 11p.m. in the centre of Thailand and into the unknown.

Two monks and a Thai female 'patient' who had a little English greeted me. They explained in broken English that check-in was not until 10a.m. the next morning, so they would do a temporary check-in; this meant basically all my belongings and clothes were taken from me.

I was body searched by the female patient, who was obviously trusted by the monks. I handed over the rest of my sleeping tablets, Xanax, antidepressants, morphine—every bit of medicine I had on me. I watched where the little monk put them into the desk drawer. A cotton pyjama-like outfit was given to me and I was allowed my flip-flops and that was it. I had nothing else, not even my toothbrush. The girl brought me to the dormitory for the girls; there was just one other girl there at the time, and she was also Thai. I was handed a blanket and shown where the toilet facilities were. I think I went into shock at this stage. I expected that everything would be basic, but it's a different story when you're reading about it at home, with the nice fuzzy feeling that Xanax gives you. Facing the stark reality was much more difficult. It was a cross between *I'm a Celebrity Get Me Out of Here* and *Big Brother*, the rough and tumble of the jungle with the security of being away from the outside world and its influences. I still had my tablets in my system and I was grateful for them at that moment, even though I knew that was the end of them once they wore off.

*

Ding a ling a ling. I woke up fast, it was like the old-fashioned burglar alarms at home: loud and intrusive. Guided by the Thai girl I got up and was handed a sweeping brush. Jesus, it was 4.30a.m. It was still dark, but I was here for a reason and that was to overcome my addiction.

I put my trust in their system, and I swept the meeting room, and the girl's dorm. Here is where I met some fellow inmates/patients. There were about 60 Thai boys, and 20 Westerners or *farangs* as we were called.

I felt lucky that I was there with a decent bunch of lads, who could all speak English. The Westerners had come from all around the world—Russia, Sweden, England, Germany, Australia, America, France and even Ireland. They made me feel so welcome and were very supportive. Even though I was the only girl in the group, they treated me fantastically well.

As I chatted to the other addicts, I realised that this was the first day in years that I hadn't taken a tablet the moment I awoke. That realisation didn't make me feel nervous. On the contrary, I felt good that I was taking control of the last part of my life that had been out of control for so long.

*

We had a timetable we had to stick to, which was kept by that flipping bell. Our day started at 4.30a.m., and went on until 9.30p.m., at which point I was locked into my room (although I had access to a secure courtyard should I need the outside air). It involved a lot of meditation, and drinking of herbal teas. One Irish lad told me there was also a time for vomiting, but I thought he was pulling my leg. Unfortunately, I was to discover the truth sooner than I liked.

By the time ten o'clock came around on the first morning, I felt as if I had been up for an entire day. It was finally time to check in and get all my stuff back, or so I thought.

I was brought to the office, where I had a chat with Phra Hans, one of the monks, who said a lot of things that made sense to me. According to him, the physical detox is only 5% of the Thamkrabok treatment. You must do the remaining 95% of the work in your mind and through your action. He also explained about the sacred vow that I was expected to take.

It's called *Sajja*, 'the vow'. Sajja is first and foremost a commitment to a (new) life of Truth and Honesty. I was making a commitment to whichever God I chose to love and myself, never to take drugs again. He said that Sajja was a sacred act that, if I believed in it, would connect me to my willpower and with something 'beyond'. Something that is far more powerful than the fight against the drugs, and it would be there for me in any moment I really wanted it strongly enough and when I was ready for it.

I took everything that he said on board, and said that I would be happy to take the vow.

Phra Hans said to me, 'Drugs are not your problem Audrey, drugs are merely the voice telling you that you have a problem.'

That struck a chord. I knew he was right and I knew I was getting rid of all my problems so I was getting rid of my addictions too. No point in clearing out your head and life if you're left with stupid dependencies that still control you.

They searched my case and didn't even give me a pack of cards, as that was gambling in their eyes. *What am I going to gamble with?* I wondered. I was given my toiletries after everything was opened, smelt and tasted. I was not allowed to have my camera, but I was delighted they let me have my pens and jotters as I kept a diary every day. I was allowed to take my books too.

I was then taken to a small temple with another lad to do our Sajja. I had no idea what I was doing, but I tried hard to focus on my desire to be free of drugs. I had to light three incense sticks and put them into a bowl, while repeating the Thai words the monk uttered as we knelt on the floor.

In the middle of this sacred ceremony, I couldn't believe it when I heard a mobile phone ringing. I was even more surprised when one of the monks answered the call. I tried not to giggle but I couldn't help it. This place was so peaceful, yet mobiles had managed to intrude in it. After that we were taken in front of Buddha and had to repeat more Thai and light more incense. That was it. I had promised never to take drugs again.

*

To my astonishment vomiting time did take place at 4.30p.m. as predicted. The men put on sarongs, and about 15 of us knelt in front of a gully, where we were expected to vomit. The medicine man came and gave us a shot glass of the most disgusting medicine, which had over 100 different herbs. He said the ingredients were a secret. This sacred medicine was to take all the toxins out of us and free us physically of the harm we had done to ourselves.

I did not even know if I believed this stuff worked. Here I was with guys who were coming off coke, methadone, heroin, tranquillisers and alcohol. I felt as if I had signed up to la-la land. I was about to puke my ring up while a bunch of inmates who had already completed the detox sang a song to us and played instruments. The song was about how we had shamed our families and were basically shitheads for ruining our lives and other people's lives with drugs. But now we had agreed to be good and stop.

I drank the disgusting mixture and then, as instructed, had to drink a bucket full of yellow-coloured warm water. I couldn't drink all the water but I drank enough to make me join the others as they vomited into the gully. I had to keep drinking the yellow water, and keep getting sick till it ran clear. What had I let myself in for?

The following day had the same routine except now I knew how horrible the puking ritual was going to be. So the whole day I could not eat, I was so nervous.

This time after vomiting I was immediately flung into withdrawals. This was the idea, apparently; it brings on your withdrawal really fast and gets it all out of your system.

I can tell you it really works. The medicine detoxes your system allowing your body to get rid of any chemicals, which means you recover quicker. Traumatic as it was, it was the best investment I ever made for myself.

At the time, though, I didn't feel close to recovery. My head was exploding, every bone in my body was sore and muscles were aching. That night I tried to get out of my room but, forgetting there was a courtyard out the back, thought I was entirely locked in. I started to freak out and banged on the door.

'Just get me to the office so I can get my morphine for the pain.'

I didn't care what they would do to me, Sajja or no Sajja, I wanted drugs to stop the agony.

The amazing thing was that people came to help. I thought I would be abandoned to work through it on my own, but an English nun got the medicine man to see me.

They spoke together quietly, and then for the first time ever, a girl was allowed sleep in the room attached to the guys' dorm. I was watched by the English nun, who in turn was watched by a monk who then was watched by another monk. To finish this chain, he was supervised by a patient. It was all very above board.

It would have been funny except for the fact I was in such pain. I hadn't been on heroin or methadone so I couldn't understand why I was in so much pain. But it was explained to me that tranquillisers were one of the hardest drugs to detox from, and had the same chemical withdrawals as heroin and methadone. I only took drugs to feel normal—not to get high—this was not fair. The pain went on for hours and I vomited into the night.

Normally monks are not allowed touch women, they cannot even hold their hands, but the medicine man can make exceptions. He spent hours massaging my head and neck while I was screaming for my morphine. He kept giving me disgusting herbal drinks, while his assistant did reflexology on my feet.

After a final bout of vomiting, I turned to thank him. The kindness, time, effort and energy he put into me was completely unselfish and it was something he did not have to do. I will never forget his words to me.

'Audrey, you are a very good person, that is why I am helping you through your pain. If I did not feel good energy from you, I would not help you.'

I believed him. He was so respected and I felt great he thought so highly of me. These people lived on a higher spiritual level than anyone I knew, and I figured he was getting good vibes from me. I was really flattered.

The next day it was the medicine man who gave the hour of vomiting. I learnt he had been a major drug lord, who had been a big drug dealer in his day, over 20 years ago. But he changed and studied herbs instead and turned his life around. He still had all the tribal gang tattoos, as well as the coolest strut you ever saw in a monk. I will never forget him. He taught me how to deal with my migraines and made me feel like a good human being.

During the next seven days I cried and truly hated the place, but I knew it was doing me good. After the seventh day I was allowed to make a phone call to my children. This was so emotional for me as I missed them desperately. I was doing this detox as much for them as I was for me, though, and I knew it was important for us all for me to be free of all drugs—prescribed and unprescribed.

I made many friends and stuck the routine for another week, but this time I was doing the singing and dancing and watching and helping others go through detox. I had not had a cigarette since I got on the plane in Dublin. Although you were allowed smoke in the compound, I chose to use this opportunity to give up for my children.

I checked out of Thamkrabok Monastery on my own after two weeks, having completed the detox. I spent a few days in a hotel four kilometres away from the monastery. It felt brilliant to have a soft bed, decent food and freedom.

Then I joined my new friends from the compound and we all spent a lovely few days in Bangkok. We were all clean and supporting each other. I knew though that I was going to be successful because I had already done a lot of work on myself before I came off drugs. I was also determined to continue counselling with the Rian group for another two years at least.

It was great to experience Thailand. I loved the tuk tuk taxis and the shopping; the cost of everything was so cheap. It is definitely a country of smiles and love. I want to go back with my children some day.

I arrived home tired—and I have to admit—scared. I was three weeks off drugs and had to face the world at home through different eyes. I did not leave the house for a few days. When I encountered my first bit of hassle since coming home, I said *how can I deal with this without my tablets?*

*

But I did. Yes, I am feeling pain stronger than I did when I was taking tablets, but I am learning to live in the present, as I was taught in the monastery.

Feel the pain, accept it and let it go. I am doing that. I am also feeling joy, though; much stronger than I ever felt.

Love is more whole and I feel I am worth even more than I did after the court case. I always loved my children, now I am really enjoying them.

I know that life will continue to throw problems at me, but I've been dealing with my day to day problems without giving in to medication.

I feel complete and whole and I am even feeling the beginning of love; a wholesome type of love. I finally feel that I can love myself; that I am someone worth loving. I continue to meditate and my migraines are controllable and much less often.

I have much to thank the monks in Thamkrabok for. I need to thank them for their understanding, care and for showing me how to live again. I know the hard work starts at home and the rest is up to me. But I have learned and gained a lot from being there, even though it was hard.

The one, most wonderful thing that I got from Thamkrabok was the ability to fall asleep naturally. After seven days of doing everything they told me, with my arms numb and pumping, finally the physical pain stopped.

It was a magical feeling being able to fall asleep on my own. It was not that I just slept once; I slept every night and have slept ever since. Not only did I sleep but I woke up at proper times without feeling groggy. Having suffered years of tormented insomnia, this is unbelievable.

I had brought my daughter's pillow from home, so I would feel close to the children, and I lay on the hard mattress and fell asleep. Night after night I slept for the first time in my life without any tossing and turning.

I had no head wrecking thoughts and no stiff tense

muscles. On nights where I lay down and didn't feel like sleeping because I was missing my children, I meditated. My body relaxed and I slept. I think it was the one gift no one has ever been able to give me. Before this, tablets were the only thing that ever worked and they left me feeling drowsy the next day.

In the evenings, I now have a natural and wonderful sleepy exhaustion. I have never ever had this and I treasure it.

*

In the past months since the court case I have become a more secure and confident person. It is not for everyone to go public in cases of abuse, but I felt that I could handle it and that the pros would outweigh the cons. I have finally let go and I no longer bear any grudges or ill feelings.

I always said that if I could save just one child or help one hurt adult then the court case would have been worth it. I now have records of countless people who have benefited from my going public.

It is so important to report a crime against children if you know of one. It has a knock-on effect, and often gives others the courage to do the same. By hiding the crime you are covering up for the paedophile. One paedophile can abuse hundreds of children in his lifetime, so by putting one away we are saving hundreds of children.

If everyone took the same attitude, we could save thousands of children. I want a child to have the confidence to walk into their home and report abuse the same way as they would if their computer game or mobile phone was stolen. Ask yourself which crime is worse, yet which is reported more often? A phone can be replaced.

In the weeks and months since the case, I have received letters from different people: from both close and distant friends wishing to express their admiration, and from victims I have never met, thanking me for making them feel like they are actually worth something after all. So many wonderful people, from all different age groups, thanking me for giving them hope.

This has reinforced the notion that I was right to confront my deepest fears, and I was right to confront my Da. I can rest easy at night knowing that he is no longer a danger to any child, and people will no longer leave him in a position of trust.

As I pen the last few lines of my story, I am feeling positive and living in the present. These days, the present is a nice place to be.

I chose to write this book to give confidence to others, to educate, and to fill a gap of understanding. To thank the gardaí, especially Peter Cooney, and to give back to the Rian group for what they have done for me.

Children are beautiful and innocent. We need to stand up for them and take responsibility for them. We set the standards for them, so we should aim high.

I think all schools should have a counsellor to deal with children's problems, no matter how small they appear to the adult. They are the only ones who can tell us what is going on in their lives.

The more we can talk about things openly, the more they will have the trust in us to confide. We laugh about toilet habits in our house. It's a great way of allowing kids to talk freely about their private parts. I trust my children are educated enough to tell me anything. I also feel confident that they know what behaviour is acceptable and what is not. But I know they are still only children and can be overpowered.

I have grown and become a more secure and independent person. I hold no grudges or ill feelings; I have at last let go. I still deal with the phobias and that will take a bit of time, but we all have burdens. I have total faith in Life to guide me in everything I do.

Epilogue

I am nearly three years down the road now and I have discovered that alcohol is also a drug, just a legal one. I did not take a Sajja against alcohol, but common sense told me addiction is addiction and any mind-altering substances do the same amount of harm. Thankfully I have never taken a drug since the monastery. I do, however, admit to smoking for two weeks during a stressful situation but I immediately got my head around it and gave them up again.

I have discovered that my positive way of looking at life is very much a Buddhist way, so I am studying and learning Buddhism and its gentle, compassionate, non-judgemental way of life and it suits me beautifully. I try my best to practise it and teach my children the same.

I got involved with 'Friends of Thamkrabok Monastery' in Google groups, an internet-based support group for anyone thinking of going to the monastery. I give advice and care along with many others who have been.

Since the Irish edition of this book was first published, I have continuously received emails and letters from adults and children who have been abused, and my life has been sent down the path of changing and educating as many people in the system as I can. A huge honour connected to this happened the day before my 43rd birthday when I was asked to do a speech at the National Counselling Service's tenth annual conference 'Transforming the Shadows' in front of hundreds of trained professionals.

Part of my speech was to get the attitudes of professionals to change and work directly on the real issues. My mother had stood by my father, and she thought that after decades of abusing me and others he would be cured after approximately six weeks of counselling. I am very very concerned about this attitude. What frightens me most is the number of girls I had witnessed my father abuse. Over at least a ten-year period it ran into the hundreds.

Our court case only managed to get six brave ladies to testify alongside me. I have spent the last few years finding answers to why more of us are not speaking up and reacting. Here are some answers from individuals who have been abused by family or close friends, which I read out as part of my speech:

1. My husband would murder him. They play golf on Sundays.
2. My husband would blame me for our marriage problems.
3. It would break my mother's heart, she is old now.
4. I went to the guards years ago but was told that the statute of limitations had run out and it was too long ago.
5. I did go but the DPP turned me down and would not take on the case.

6. I have a statement in the gardaí should anyone else come forward about the same person, I am not enough on my own.

7. Audrey I had a statement in the gardaí in the Bridewell in relation to your dad, and it was only when I saw you on the news I wondered why I was not called. I contacted the gardaí and they said it was not on the system. Though they found my statement. I was informed I cannot take a case now.

8. Stigma, I could not live with the stigma. Abuse victims abuse, everyone believes that, I wanted to be a nurse.

9. I was told by my family not to put that good man down. How dare I make such accusations.

10. I was told no man would ever want me by my mother, I was damaged goods so keep quiet.

11. I was not believed. I did tell.

12. It was my fault I never said no.

13. My father depended on my abuser for his job so I was not allowed say anything though they did keep me away from him.

14. I was told it was his way of loving me. There was no harm.

15. I had no evidence.

16. My mother threatened to commit suicide if I did tell anyone.

17. I was emotionally blackmailed, in speaking out I would hurt many instead of just the one, me.

18. I have not been able to say the words out loud to anyone.

19. I did go to counselling and my counsellor asked me did I have any feelings sexually towards children. I don't I

swear, I never have. I never went back to counselling as I felt the lowest of scum for being asked such a question. I have never spoke about it to anyone till you Audrey.

20. My sisters said it didn't happen to them so therefore they maintained it didn't happen to me.

21. I love my dad. I hate what he did. But I could not put him away. I emigrated so he cannot come near my children.

22. I said nothing, I thought it was just me that was the bad one, now my three-year-old daughter has told me she was abused by her granddad. What do I do now? I did this to her. I am to blame. I really thought it was me and not him.

23. When I was younger he said he would kill my little brother. I am older now but the fear of him hurting someone I love if I said anything haunts me.

24. I just want to get on with my life and by bringing it into my adult life he has won. I won't let him take the time I have left. I want to show him he has had no effect on me. (I might add this was said by a man who had three broken marriages and was now an alcoholic.)

25. I don't want the world knowing my business. Someone will find out even if I remain anonymous.

26. I cannot deal with it, I have tried counselling, it's not for me. I don't have the nerve.

27. He is old now and sick, what's the point?

28. It would kill my parents, I do not want to hurt them.

29. My siblings said just get on with it, it's over and what would I achieve.

30. My siblings said this will bring the family down, I don't have that right to hurt everyone. They are sorry it happened

but our kids will be bullied in school if everyone found out.

31. My in-laws hate me enough anyway, this would give them great pleasure finding out I was related to an abuser. They are always putting my family down.

32. I work with children, if this ever got out, I fear the consequences. I love my job and I adore kids.

33. Ashamed of what happened.

34. Ashamed of what people would say because I never spoke up before now.

35. Ashamed because up until five years ago I spoke and laughed with my uncle and people saw me. How can I say it happened and expect them to believe me. I have faced it. I cannot do any more. I keep my three-year-old son away from functions he attends.

36. I was slapped and told what an awful child I was. The filth that came out of my mouth.

37. I spoke up and every problem that arises I got the blame as I was the damaged one. I stopped bringing it to people's attention and don't talk about it.

38. I cannot take the pity I receive. Like I'm only an abused person and not a person who was abused as well as being a good father.

39. I have too much to lose with my family. I couldn't be alone. It's better all round if I don't.

40. I think I would break if I spoke about it.

Time and again, it is fear about what others think that stops these men and women coming forward. Too often, it is fear about what family members will think.

When a mother chooses to stay with a father, or any family member chooses to stay with a predator, it's not an informed choice if they are never told the reality of the situation. After communicating with many families over the last few years I have discovered it is common for them to not really know what the abuser in their midst is really like, which is why survivors can wait 20 or 30 years to speak out. The spouse who naively serves as protector of the criminal, emotionally blackmails the victim they are related to. She also gives the opportunist plenty more opportunity to abuse other innocent little children. It is the safety of children that should come first.

*

So how can we make things safer for children? When a partner finds out they are living with a suspected abuser or confessed abuser, she usually needs support in the form of counselling. But counselling cannot just be about building self-confidence and dealing with anxieties. It is society's obligation to make sure that mothers are fully informed about the personality type of abusers – of their behaviours which include manipulation, compulsions, dangers, grooming. Abusers can look normal when they do lunch, walk in the park and at any occasions and celebrations they attend. Family members should also be made very aware of what it's like for the victim, the long-lasting damaging effects.

I knew that prosecuting my dad and naming and shaming him was the only way to stop him because he was protected every which way he turned by our backward culture. I had a fire inside me amongst all the heartbreak and I persevered. I want to stress this is not a responsibility that victims should carry. But if we reconditioned society and shed the shame and stigma of being abused it would not carry as much weight.

My ultimate goal is not to hurt or be vengeful, but to protect children. To allow them to walk into their homes or schools and safely say a person *tried* to touch, hurt, abuse, use them *before it becomes an act.* Or, if the worst happens, that they can speak out after the first time and that it ends there and then. We need to teach children not to be manipulated, so that the abuser has no power.

In Ireland the church and other institutions are being blamed, and rightly so, for covering up and protecting themselves and their reputation first and foremost, and not the beautiful children in their care. Over and over this is mirrored within families. I have heard individuals rip priests apart while they sit and watch the news knowing they are doing the exact same within their own family. If their family member was abused by a priest, stranger or someone they are not emotionally involved with they would be up there and behind them and wanting the perpetrator punished.

I have always said would you let a dangerous dog run around a housing estate knowing it can attack a child. Why would we allow an adult? The scars of abuse do not heal as easily as a dog bite. Would you hand your keys of your brand new car to a stranger or leave them in the ignition outside your house? Why do we not protect our children in equal terms? We have to stop putting them in danger that lurks because of all the cover-ups.

I believe the whole matter of child abuse needs to be approached in a more holistic way so we are not just treating those who have been abused but take every step to make sure our children are protected in the future. Of course the survivor needs to stay in control of his or her journey, that goes without saying. But the gardaí must liaise better with counsellors and social services, and everyone involved – brothers, sisters, mothers, fathers, husbands, wives – should be educated to the seriousness of the crime; the compulsions the offenders have, how dangerous and likely they are to reoffend; and how the healing of survivors can be accelerated by the reaction and support of the family and surrounding contacts in their life. I knew this instinctively, but I wished someone had taken my family and told them.

*

After my speech, the applause from the audience went on and on. I was overwhelmed and speechless, I think I went into shock. All day I was approached by counsellors, directors and professionals, given cards and congratulations. It was the most surreal experience and I was so proud to be part of it.

This event was made even more special as I had my wonderful man at my side who I had met and fallen deeply in love with. He is spiritual, loving, understanding, kind, positive and totally supportive of me. I might add he is rough around the edges in a very sexy way and very very handsome. If I was to describe a hero for my ending, he would be it. I have never ever felt love like this. He is the only person in my adult life who I trust and makes me feel so special and cherished. Our love is spiritual, physical and emotional. I can give it and receive it without question. It's something so new to me, that I have never done before. I still have a lot to learn and I always will continue to improve.

I meditate and pray often and it is an important part of my life. Everything I have asked for I have been given.

Before I begin the next chapter of my life, the following quote sums up my feelings about this book, and about life in general.

Ephesians 4:29: 'Do not use harmful words but only helpful words, the kind that build up and provide what is needed, so that what you say will do good to those who hear you.'

Acknowledgements

To the other girls who were brave enough to bare their souls, find the courage and speak out, your country should thank you. I am grateful and I admire you all. You are heroines.

I wish to thank Christine Buckley, founder of the Aishlinn Centre, who I hold as a magnificent glowing inspiration. She has opened up many doors, making it easier for me.

Thanks to my friend Mary, for everything over the last 14 years, and for travelling to Ireland for my father's sentencing.

I wish to thank my godmother and my uncle from Greystones for their consistent love and support. I also want to give my love to my aunt and uncle in Crumlin.

To Debbie and Brian, Harry and ViVi, who took care of and protected Tyrone and Robin during the court days. Long-term friends.

To the girls in Celbridge for their continuous love and

support, thanks for not forgetting me even though I am not great at phoning.

Thanks Michelle for the ear and for coming to the trial with me.

Thanks also to the girls in Virginia, Cavan, who looked after me and my kids through the months in 2006 when I was sick. You saved me. You who slag me over my lackadaisical ways and lateness with smiling faces.

To the 'Castle Lodge' bed and breakfast for treating me like a princess. Their kindness, empathy and warmth makes them the best B & B in the world. I always knew I was a princess in real life. They just merely showed me how it felt. It felt good and in such an emotional time.

Thanks to Aslan for their song 'Crazy World'. I know how to protect the kids now.

Special thanks to Christy Dignan from Aslan for contacting me, a nobody; yet from that phone call came a life changing experience and I felt like somebody. You are a man with a good soul. Not many musicians take the time to look after an ordinary Irish girl like Christy did.

SPECIAL ACKNOWLEDGEMENTS

I am deeply grateful to Detective Peter Cooney, who spent years working on my case and never gave up, as frustrating as it got. He is a kind and understanding man. I trust him. Thanks to Mary Rose Gearty, the barrister who worked on the case, for a job well done.

To Essie, my ever loyal and supportive counsellor in the Rian Group run by the Health Board. You built me up and helped me to have the faith in myself I have today. It is my own feelings that count and I direct them in a positive and loving way towards others.

To my brothers, thanks so much for everything.

I have to give complete thanks to the Thamkrabok Monastery in Thailand. It was traumatic; a massive endurance test, which pushed me through boundaries I never thought I could go to, and I'm proud I have. It was a huge life-changing experience in such a positive way. Thank you for the many gifts I left there with, most of all, the gift of sleep. It was the best investment I ever made for my children and myself.

Thanks to my new friend Mae Shee Rambhai Singhsumalee, the Medicine Man; a very special man and all the monks and nuns who cared for me and who asked for nothing back. My friend Charlie who kept me sane throughout my stay, and all the patients who were there during my time: thank you for still keeping in touch.

To my friend Eugene, who is a missionary priest. I have known him since I was three years old and his words have given me great peace.

To my publishers, Maverick House, who treated me with respect and care. To Bridgette Rowland, who painstakingly read my book and was forever complimentary. To Jean Harrington, who made sense of a jumble of emotions, and asked the right questions.

To Michael Kealey of William Fry Solicitors, thanks so much for his preparation work on the manuscript prior to publication.

I would also like to acknowledge the effect that Sorcha McKenna, another child abuse victim, had on me. When

I saw her going public about the abuse she suffered at the hands of her father, it set everything in motion for me. I realised that if she could do it, then I could also do it. Thank you for your bravery, Sorcha.

I thank everyone who has been part of my life no matter what the situation; it has all benefited me and I have learned from every experience in a good way.

'Smile and look at life and everyone in it through angel's eyes. Make sure the next thing you say to someone brings you peace.'

Happy Being Me

I am a boy; I'm nine years old,
I might look normal and so I'm told,
But I've a syndrome called Tourettes,
The older I grow, the worse it gets.
It makes me run, jump and kick, it even makes me get
    very sick.
Sometimes it makes me talk and shout 'YES.'
It really does fill me up with stress.
It makes me want to twirl around,
It even makes me do a silly sound.
It makes me blink and crinkly my nose,
My lips go into a funny pose.
I get so tired my body moves all night,
I get so scared my Tourettes gives me a fright!
People point and tease, that makes me sad,
The Tourettes I have is not at all bad. I feel very special,
Because it makes me understand,
That if I see a person with a problem,
I'll always give them a hand.
So please remember when you laugh,
And tease at people like me,
You can't tell the future, it could be you or your family!

by Tyrone Ward